MW01249203

I AM FROM

An Americana Narrative

Judith Fawley (signature)

Judith Fawley

Copyright © 2017 Author Judith G. Fawley
All rights reserved.
ISBN: 1539346854
ISBN-13: 978-1539346852

DEDICATION

This book is for my children – Kimberly, James and Jefferson – so you never forget your grandparents, or that your mother was once a kid.

ACKNOWLEDGMENTS

Thanks to the Portfolio Society – Diane Skelton *(The Gumbo Diaries, Mississippi and Beyond)*, Victoria Franks *(The Aroma of Coffee)*, Susan Feathers *(Threshold)*, and Jeannie Zokan *(The Existence of Pity)*, for their encouragement to just-finish-the-book.

Special thanks to my sister, Jo Ellen, for jogging my memory when I'd run out of juice. My appreciation to both sisters, Jo and June, for providing a lifetime of material.

Extraordinary edits of text and photos by Diane J. Skelton. Through generous sharing of her time and many talents, Diane salvaged my memoir.

Book cover by gifted Victoria E. Franks.

In addition, a fond thank you to Jackson, Missouri, a great place to grow up.

TABLE OF CONTENTS

CONTENTS

I Am From

By Judith Fawley © 2012

I am from a rural community with rock solid values and church dinners-on-the-dirt.

I am from collie dogs that raced free in the meadows and litters of kittens that magically appeared in the grain shed.

I am from autumn hog killing, wheat threshing and rides to school in a horse-drawn wagon insulated with straw.

I am from families and equipment passing from one farm to another until everyone's smoke house and barn loft was full.

I am from makeshift tables laden with hearty, abundant meals and gallons of tea.

I am from mule-pulled plows and cows milked twice a day.

I am from biscuits for breakfast, cornbread for dinner and whatever was left for supper.

I am from Eastern Star meetings and Masonic Lodge halls.

I am from bacon and mashed potatoes smothered in gravy five times a week.

I am from swims in ice cold creeks and prowls in the woods for wild onions and hickory nuts.

I am from bedtime at dusk because it's too expensive to burn the smoky coal-oil lamps.

I am from boxes cooled with blocks of ice and battery-operated radios used only for Cardinal baseball and The Lone Ranger.

I am from heating irons on the cook stove and boiling laundry in a cauldron over a fire near the garden.

I am from frugal management of resources and squandering of none.

I am from homegrown canned tomatoes, green beans, peaches, apples and plums.

I am from Homecomer's each September when carnival rides and barkers descended on all three blocks of town.

I am from a one-room school house with thirteen students in eight grades.

I am from attending school as soon as I could walk two miles to get there.

I am from napping on the desk seat when the teacher called my sister up to recite.

I am from baths in the rinse water and hanging clothes in the attic during winter.

I am from playing with baby chicks in the brooder house and exploring the rabbit hutch.

I am from pumping the cistern for a cool drink and slipping a hand beneath warm chickens to retrieve eggs.

I am from churning to make butter kept cool in the spring house and chasing down a hen for Sunday dinner.

I am from Saturday afternoon dime double-features and five-cent ice cream cones.

I am from a farmer's daughter and a professional gambler.

I am from generations of English, German and Dutch ancestors.

I am from a blind street sweeper who was part Cherokee Indian.

I am from a young bride left to raise her six brothers when their
mother died.

I am from two siblings - one that taught me to read and one that
taught me to fight.

I am from playing Roy Rogers and Dale Evans during recess with
Alta Faye.

I am from living in Jackson, Missouri, city of beautiful homes,
churches, schools, and parks.

I am from listening to summer night concerts when my dad sang and
played his guitar on the side porch steps.

I am from lying across the bed reading *Little House on the Prairie*
aloud to Mom while she worked at the bedroom sewing machine.

I am from classroom prayer, Pledge of Allegiance, marching band,
and home economics class.

I am from steadfast people, loyal, brave and persevering.

I am from playing war with neighborhood children in the dirt gullies
of undeveloped streets.

I am from Christian church services and Vacation Bible School.

I am from creating my own world in the upstairs junk room with a
toy railroad, farm set and building blocks.

I am from rocking chairs and a grandma who warmed my clothes by
the kitchen stove in winter.

JUDITH FAWLEY

I am from crinoline petticoats that trapped grasshoppers within
during lunch hours.

I am from walking where ever I wanted to go and knowing the name
of everyone, and their dog.

I am from the library, city hall, church basements, Jones' Drug Store,
the IGA and A&P.

I am from a work in progress with rough edges
and unfinished dreams.

The Everette Linebarger Family
Daddy, Judy and Mom in front, Jo and June in back. Circa 1946.

JUDITH FAWLEY

I am from a rural community with rock solid values and church dinners-on-the-dirt.

When we moved to Jackson in 1950, the population was around 3,700. Located in the boot heel of Missouri, our large city was Cape Girardeau, seven miles away. It was named by Pierre Laclede for his officer, Lieutenant Girardeau, who died there. Laclede went on to establish the fur-trading village that became St. Louis - 120 miles north of Jackson. I spent my first seven years between the small

Methodist Church at Sedgewickville, MO. Photo 2016.

towns Millersville and Sedgewickville, seven and fifteen miles from Jackson. At the only intersection in Sedgewickville, the Methodist and Lutheran Churches are located on opposite corners. The Lutherans owned a cemetery but had no church building; the Methodists owned a church building but had no cemetery. With great cooperation, each group used the other's asset for their common needs. There was a joint Sunday service at the church and no religious qualification for burial in the cemetery. Originally, parishioners arrived via horse and buggy.

Methodist Church with Lutheran Church and cemetery in distance.
Photo 2016.

In that small rural area, everyone knew everyone else. They had children in the same school they had attended, belonged to the same social groups, shared harvest chores and supported the mutual functions. When someone needed help, these were the folks that came to their rescue. It might be milking the cows, plowing a field, providing a meal or sitting up all night with a sick neighbor so the family could get some rest. It was a compassionate, nurturing community of similar people.

The church was always unlocked, as all churches were in those days. It was unimaginable that anyone would enter a holy sanctuary for the purposes of destruction or theft. Houses of worship were respected for what they were: places to commune and converse with God.

After church, folks often stayed on for a "dinner-on-the-dirt." Quilts and blanket were spread on the grass beneath shade trees and picnic lunches of cold fried chicken were
shared. Tea was transported in glass jars and dishes were packed between towels or clean rags with great care. Glasses were equally wrapped and included my favorite, which had previously contained jelly. My grandparents on Daddy's side met at one such dinner.

The building adjacent church where the Limbaugh School Reunion was held. Photo 2016.

Grandpa, James Edward Linebarger, was part Cherokee Indian, although it was Grandma, Ida Mae Cook, who looked Native American. They had seven children: Lloyd, who died when he was about two, Ermine (Uncle Limey), Eula, Howard, Oma, Everette (Daddy), and Golda. Lloyd was buried in the Lutheran Cemetery in an unmarked grave; they couldn't afford a marker. At the time, they knew he was located four steps from the metal entrance gate.

Mom often pointed to that particular area and said, "Daddy's baby brother, Loy, is somewhere over there."

It was customary to visit a loved one's grave on Memorial Day, as well as other special occasions of the particular family. Remnants

Limbaugh School Reunion. Jo is on the left end behind the walker, and June is in the back row near Jo.

from previous decorations were gathered and deposited in trash bins. The graves were weeded and groomed. A caretaker mowed the grass, but often flowers were planted or bouquets were placed in front of the tombstone by family members. I learned cemetery etiquette early: never tread on the graves or sit on a gravestone.

Lynn Haas, the fellow who had the family grave lots just above the plot for Mom, teased that she'd spend eternity smelling his feet. She would shake her head and fuss at him, just as he wanted.

My folks, both sets of grandparents, numerous aunts, uncles and cousins have joined Lloyd in their final resting place in the Lutheran Cemetery, though not one was Lutheran.

The auxiliary building where we attended Bible School until 1950 still stands. Photo 2016.

Judy, age 13. Jackson.

I am from a farmer's daughter and a professional gambler

Mom completed high school in Jackson and went to business school in Cape Girardeau where she learned typing, bookkeeping, and shorthand. She lived with Caroline and Lilli Seabaugh, T.J.

From left: Lela "Buck" Drum, Glendell Drum and Mom in Cape Girardeau, MO. Circa 1917.

Seabaugh's mother and sister, while she went to school. Later she moved in with Aunt Grace and went to work for T.J., who was a little kin, on Pearl Street in Cape Girardeau. Pearl Street ended at the shoe factory intersection of Main Street. Seabaugh's Store, a general store or mercantile, that sold canned and fresh food, meats, fabric, pantry staples, clothing, garden items, tools, first aid materials, matches, etc.

On the other side of my family, Grandpa and Grandma Linebarger lived in Cape Girardeau, on Pearl Street, across from Seabaugh's. Grandma ran a charge account at the store, through the kindness of T.J.'s heart, as there was no such thing then. T.J. visited Grandma one day and explained that her account had reached the enormous sum of $150 and he wanted her to send one of her boys to work for him to pay it off. Uncle Howard announced in no uncertain terms that he would not be doing that work. Everette (Daddy) just said, "I'll do it, Mom."

Mom is the fourth stylish girl from the right.

Each morning before school, evenings after school and Saturdays till 5:00, Daddy worked at Seabaugh's. Once a week, he'd swing a hundred-pound bag of pinto beans over his shoulder to carry to Grandma. And, he met Mom, who was four years his senior, while working there.

Mom expected to work for a corporation but T.J. needed someone to work at the store so she stayed there. She was employed from age twenty to age twenty-six, making twelve dollars a week.

Every Monday, T.J. would order three dressed hogs. On Thursday or Friday, he'd order two more. They would smoke the shoulders and bacon. T.J. had Daddy start going through the spice cabinet to experiment making sausage. If it didn't taste like Daddy wanted, he used a little something different next time. The salami Daddy made was so good customers would line up and wait until it was ready.

On Fridays, T.J. went the bank and exchange several hundred dollars for small bills and change. The shoe factory employees were

The milk bottles from Seabaugh's Store. Photo 2016.

paid by check at the end of each week. Most of them came to the store to cash their check and buy weekend groceries. Mom and Daddy (who were yet to be married), were asked to stay until 9:00 those nights to see to the needs of this clientele. Daddy ran the deli counter and cut meat; Mom tended to general merchandise sales.

Since they worked through dinner, they were permitted to make a sandwich from the deli case and have a beverage, usually a bottle of milk. About ten years before my dad passed away in 1990, he gave me a collection of one-dozen milk bottles, saved from those

Friday nights when my folks worked late. For many years, the bottles sat on the open beams above my kitchen counters. I filled them with colored Easter grass and plastic eggs and tied raffia around the necks to make them attractive.

Mom sold shoes, stocked shelves, and cut fabric. Potatoes, beans, and sugar, as well as other bulk items, came in hundred-pound bags that had to be broken down to five or ten pound bags.

Mom sold shoes, stocked shelves, and cut fabric. Potatoes, beans, and sugar, as well as other items, came in hundred-pound bags that had to be broken down to five or ten pound bags.

An anniversary celebration was being held on Good Hope near the movie theater. Mom and Daddy decided to go together. At square dances, Mom liked to dance with the caller. Her shoes had cardboard soles and she had danced holes in very pair. Daddy didn't know how to dance at all but by the end of the evening, he was dancing.

Daddy didn't have spending money when he was a teenager because it was all applied to Grandma's debt at the store. However, on those rare occasions he did have two nickels to rub together, he Sundays, but on the other days of the week, Daddy learned to play cards very, very well.

When a bunch of the fellows would be holed-up playing pinochle for money, which was illegal, a lookout was posted at the door watching for the police. The lookout earned five cents from each pot. They played cribbage, pool, checkers, anything they could bet on. When there was a dispute regarding the rules or the way a hand played out, they fought. Daddy and another young man once fought in the rain. By the time they finished in exhaustion, they were covered with mud, and all Daddy had left on was his belt. They were fighting in an empty lot near the shoe factory. When Daddy glanced up, every window was crowded with workers watching the fight. They were lucky it was muddy.

Before they wed, Daddy liked a girl Mom always referred to as "Daddy's little blonde." He called her one Saturday afternoon and she wanted to go to the movies. The movie cost ten cents each and all Daddy had was two nickels. She pouted and made him feel badly that he couldn't afford to show her a fun time. After he got off the phone, Mom, who had overheard, piped up that she had a dime, so they went to the show.

It was cold so they would walk from Pearl to Good Hope then run all the way to Broadway to the movie. They had to walk past a cemetery that Mom didn't especially like, so she watched carefully as they passed it.

The next week, the blonde suggested seeing the movie. Daddy said he'd seen it. She demanded, "With whom?" He said, "With Pete." (Mom's nickname.) That was it - bye bye, Blondie.

When Mom and Daddy's engagement was announced in the local newspaper, (Rita Looney to wed Everette Linebarger), people would come into the store and complain to T. J., "Why, I thought Everette was

That picture of Daddy.

11

going to marry Pete." Few people knew her by her given name of Rita.

It was Mom's intention to work at the store until Aunt Grace's youngest daughter graduated from high school, so she and Daddy dated for five years. Finally the youngest niece, Glendell, graduated and the next weekend married a sailor named Stacy Gearing. Ticked Mom off! Here she'd waited all that time for Glen to graduate and the little brat went and got married before she did.

When I was eight or nine, we were with Mom at an Eastern Star meeting when a lady walked in. Mom said my sisters and I were slumped on the bench in boredom, when she leaned over and whispered, "There's Daddy's little blonde." Our backbones went rigid as we craned our respective necks to get a good look at this often-referenced person (in a teasing way). It was like sighting a Yeti or Big Foot.

As I recall the glimpse of Daddy's little blonde, whose name was Myrtle, was that she was petite and light haired, or it may have been gray by then. She had a picture someone made of Daddy. Although she was married numerous times, the picture stayed on her bedroom dresser.

When Myrtle became terminally ill, she had the picture delivered to Mom. Aunt Oma found that out and made sure Aunt Eula knew it, which totally pissed Eula off. Aunt Eula enjoyed other's envy of her possessions.

Grandma and Grandpa Looney were helping Aunt Grace raise her three girls, Lela Oma Drum, Sarah Edith Avery, Glendell Vesta Gearing, so Mom always took her salary home and gave it to Grandma. When Mom married, Grandma Looney gave her a bankbook for the account Grandma had opened in Mom's name that had $400 in it.

Several years after the move to Jackson, Mom took a job at the shoe factory and rode in a carpool. A carpool was usually five persons, each driving one day of the week, picking up and returning the other four passengers. Every June 13th she'd tell them, "Tomorrow is my wedding anniversary; they'll put the flags out along the high-

Everette Lee Linebarger and Rita "Pete" Marie Looney on their wedding day, June 14, 1936, Cape Girardeau, Missouri. The flowers Mom carried were Sweet Peas from the farm. She transplanted some when we moved to Jackson, where they still grow along the side of the house.

13

way." Sure enough, it happened. (June 14th is National Flag Day.)

Following their marriage, Daddy would sometimes disappear for days, gambling. He rarely lost but it frustrated Mom that he was gone so often to where ever. He told me the last time he gambled he came home with over $300 in his pocket – a small fortune.

When he opened the door to his darkened house, he discovered that his wife had taken their two babies and all their furnishings back home. Daddy followed Mom to the farm, where he worked for the next grueling fourteen years. He still occasionally played penny-ante poker with neighbors, but his Diamond Jim days were behind him.

A few days before their 50th wedding anniversary celebration, Daddy took me aside and asked me to go buy a gold chain necklace for him to give Mom. My husband and I went to a jewelry store

Mom and Daddy's 50th wedding anniversary. Jackson, 1986. It doesn't show in this photo, but the gold necklace is in place.

in Cape that had previously treated us very nicely. I explained my mission, and the clerk had me lean forward. He proceeded to place about twenty gold chains around my neck. He said, "Go home and show them to your dad. Bring back what he doesn't want tomorrow." A trusting action unlikely to occur these days.

Daddy selected a lovely simple necklace, and I returned all the others that same night! When he placed it around Mom's neck, he said, "If you take this off, I'll have to paddle you."

Mom smiled at him and said, "Don't worry, Pop, you won't have to spank me." (As if he ever would.)

The St. Louis Iron Mountain and Southern Railway train in Jackson had an engine and several passenger cars. It traveled about five miles then returned to town. They had a popcorn machine and a piano for entertainment. My children, Jeff and Kim, were with my

Mom circa 1928.

husband Gene and me.

Mom and Daddy were giddy with all kids and many grandkids coming and making such a fuss over them. It was delightful to watch them enjoy the ride. That day Kim discovered that Jeff could make her laugh and they actually became friends.

A reception took place in the Methodist Church basement and all the relatives attended. Jeff had needed a suit and we found one at Penney's at Chapel Hill Mall in Akron. It was an Italian-made suit on clearance because the trousers had a twenty-eight inch waist – it fit him perfectly. I have a photo of him serving punch, looking very elegant. He was fifteen and already six-feet tall.

As the folks opened cards of congratulation, money fell out. That was unexpected and delighted them. We girls bought them a microwave oven. After some hemming and hawing about being afraid of it, they used it a lot. We replaced it many years later and Gene put the old one at the curb for trash pickup. As we drove away to travel home to Ohio, I looked in the rear-view mirror and saw Mom dragging the microwave by the cord toward the basement.

Newspaper account of the anniversary party.

Mom

Daddy with Jo, next to Mom and June. On the farm circa 1939. The pipe from the downspouts to the cistern is visible on the right side of the first photo.

I am from autumn hog killing, wheat threshing and rides to school in a horse-drawn wagon insulated with straw.

Wheat threshing and hog killing were cooperative endeavors as both equipment and manpower rotated from farm to farm for two weeks in the fall. Since electric power lines had not been extended into the country, refrigeration wasn't available, so beef was never killed. Hog killing provided fresh pork that was preserved by salting or smoking. Each farm had a smoke house where hams and bacon slabs were hung for curing.

Available equipment for the task at hand. Circa 1940's.

Usually the entire family traveled with the work equipment. Mom took vegetables, hens, fruits, dishes, chairs, silverware and glass jars for beverages. While the men worked, the women cooked. It was-strenuous labor for everyone. Tea was brewed by the gallons, biscuits and cornbread baked, chickens killed, plucked and fried, sweet potatoes peeled and candied, corn-on-the-cob, shucked and boiled, white potatoes whipped, and salads drizzled with hot bacon grease.

Apples, pears, peaches, and whatever else was in season, was added to heavily laden tables.

During one dinner, a man requested that the lettuce be passed so he could get another spoonful. It was served in a large round metal dishpan that was covered with dents and dings from years of use. As each man took it to pass it on, he ladled a serving on his own plate and asked, "A spoonful like that?" By the time it reached the one that had requested another serving, the basin was empty. No fear, the kitchen was sending out more.

All this food preparation was completed in a kitchen that probably reached near one hundred degrees. At that time, there was no running water inside houses. Open window cross-ventilation was the only relief for the sweating women cooking on the hot surfaces. A wood-burning stove and a crowd of mature cooks in each other's way, yes, it got hot in there! I never heard raised or angry voices coming from the bustling, sweltering room.

Tables were created by using sawhorses covered with planks. If the wife was the persnickety kind, a bed sheet was spread over the planks as a make-do tablecloth.

Water was drawn from a well or cistern. Coming from underground depths, it might stay cool for a few minutes but would soon yield to the outdoor heat and grow tepid. Milk was served at whatever the temperature might be.

On one occasion, Mom opened a kitchen cabinet door and found a plump golden chicken breast that a wife had secreted there for her husband. This was not the first instance the wife had hidden a choice portion for her man. Mom took the plate, walked outside and presented it to Daddy. I don't know if she even tried to look innocent as she did it, but it did put a stop to the hoarding.

It was long ago, but I clearly remember slipping my grubby hand beneath the cloth cover over a platter of sweet potatoes and making off with a still warm stolen treat.

The animals were fed, watered and rested while the men ate. Tools were cleaned and sharpened for the afternoon work.

When the farmers returned to their own homes, livestock had to be fed, cows milked, eggs gathered, chickens shooed into the hen house, supper cooked and children put to bed. All chores needed to be accomplished before it was totally dark.

We children never witnessed the actual hog killing and didn't really understand what all the work was about. It was my favorite time of year as I got to see and play with friends. We had to stay out of the kitchen and everyone else's way. At our farm we played with my flame-shaped tree root and chased each other with fresh pig's tails cut from the dearly departed.

After a pig was killed, the hams, shoulders and bacon were salted down or hung in the smoke house. Cracklings were made from the skin. Everything that was left was put in the kettle over the fire outside and boiled down. Mom made soap from the pig renderings with added lye. It would solidify in a pan into a solid rectangle about

Judy and Jo playing in the Jackson front yard. Circa 1955.

two inches thick. She would cut it into squares and slice it with a paring knife into the boiling iron caldron on washdays.

When autumn had passed and winter snows set in, a wagon would sometimes stop at our driveway. A team of steaming horses with clouds of vapor rising from their nostrils pulled the wagon which was full of loose straw. We children piled into the wagon and covered ourselves with the meager insulation for the slow two-mile ride to the schoolhouse. This luxury conveyance was only provided if walking to school was not possible.

My mother had attended this same elementary school. She told us that sometimes the snow was so high she could bite mouthfuls from either side of a path without bending over. I have no idea who created that path to the school building, probably Grandpa Looney.

Once a soaking rainstorm complete with lightning broke out while we were walking to school. A Greyhound bus stopped beside us and opened its door. Jo, June and I jumped in, grateful for the reprieve from the weather, and were shortly deposited at the front door of our school building. It was miraculous that the bus stopped, and it never happened again.

Daddy with Jo.

22

HAYMOWING

Hay mowing. Notice the barn in the background.

When it was time to mow, excitement ran high since making hay was as labor intensive as wheat thrashing. After the wheat was thrashed, the left over by-product was straw. Straw was used for bedding in the barn and for stuffing our mattresses once a year. In winter, a feather bed (a comforter made of blue-striped ticking full of fowl feathers) was spread over the mattress. We were not permitted to play on the straw stacks because the weight of our bodies would break it down and you would end up with a flat mattress. When the mattress was fresh, we spent prickly nights on them since the hay ends poked through the mattress and bugs captured within were still alive.

Alfalfa was planted for hay, which was fed to the farm animals. We had several hay fields which were mowed when it reached a height of twelve to twenty inches. If conditions were right, it could be mowed twice a year. The mowed hay was formed into rows in the field and left to dry. Often it was fluffed with a pitchfork to get air through it and accelerate the drying. If it was damp when it was put into the hayloft, it would mold.

Mom in a tobacco field in Zenith, Missouri, Circa 1930.

The circuit for hay was the same as wheat thrashing. Men, animals and equipment passed from farm to farm helping with the harvest. Dried hay was thrown by pitchfork onto a hay wagon. Men on top stomped the hay to keep it steady on the wagon. If a man on the ground saw a wiggly serpent as the hay was hurled onto the wagon, he'd yell, "Snake." The men on top would jump off, kill the snake and start all over again. Mom worked in the fields like a hired hand with Grandpa Looney. She never liked working with the pitchfork because she feared a snake would fall on her. Once again, the farmwomen would converge to prepare and serve the noon meal.

The hay wagon was pulled to the barn by a team of horses or mules and parked at the back where two large doors on the upper level were opened. The hayfork was passed down to the wagon and the tines were secured around a mound of hay. An inch-and-one-half thick

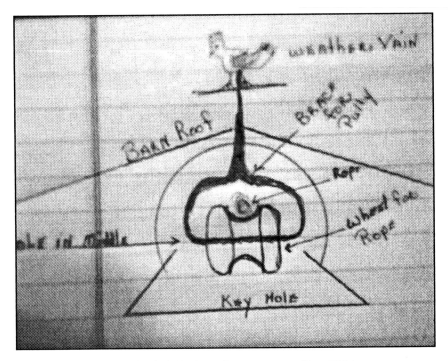

Barn keyhole Jo drew from memory. Circa 2014.

a two-inch groove in it. The rope went through a key hole, an opening of six by ten inches long and rounded at the top, in the barn wall, and then traveled on down to the ground on the other side. Another team of work animals waited there for the delivery of the filled fork.

When the fork was full, the second team of animals pulled the rope through the barn, lifting the hayfork until it was positioned above where the hay was to be dropped. A signal was given for everyone to stand clear and a trigger rope was pulled that released the tines of the fork and the straw was
dropped into the loft. In seconds, the slacked rope on the outside of the barn was pulled back through the key hole and made tight by the hay fork, ready for the next load.

At feeding time, hay was pitched through a four-foot square in the loft floor to the lower level of the barn. From there it was carried by pitchfork or wheelbarrow to assorted mangers for horses, mules and cows. The weathervane on the barn roof was the top bolt to hold the hayfork in place.

No children were allowed inside the barn lot during the time the loft was being replenished with hay. Unfortunately, no one noticed innocent Carol Seabaugh, a second grade classmate whose family was helping, when she entered the lot. She made the mistake of taking hold of the loft rope. Carol must not have heard or recognized the warning of imminent release. The speed of the rope as it zipped through her hand was so intense it burned off three of her fingers.

Jo and June were the men's water carriers. It took both of them to carry a gallon bucket full of fresh cistern water to the barn lot. In turn, each man drank a dipper of water and my sisters went back for more.

The barn was located just beyond the pond, which was the drinking water source for the animals. In hot weather, it was not unusual to see the cows standing in the pond, the water just covering their udders.

Walking into the barn brought on high anticipation and exciting tension, anything could happen. There would be a sudden flurry of sound from the rapidly flapping wings of disturbed pigeons. Wayward feathers would waft soundlessly though the spec-filled air to

June 9, Judy 3, and Jo 10, on the farm with a new crop of kittens. 1948.

the floor. Whisper thin shafts of sunlight stole in between boards onto the floor, creating a strobe effect. The pungent smell of animal waste was omnipresent and it was dusty dim inside. If the wind was out of the East, it moaned through the gaps in the barn siding and made leather harnesses creak as they swayed on their hooks. Weathered boards groaned with its motion. It was another world and a fantastic place to play. The hayloft was usually our destination for adventure.

There were bales of hay beneath the eaves of the barn. With great effort, Jo and June moved and stacked the bales to form rooms. Our play table and chairs were moved up there, along with dolls, tea sets and toys. Even a child's rocking chair.

The hay fork, which hung from the top of the barn on a rope, was extremely dangerous. Children were cautioned not to play around it because if it fell, it would impale the child. Jo and June would memorize how the fork rope was bound to a post, untie it and we would swing on it in huge circles inside the barn, around the hay fork, never directly beneath it. When we tired, they retied the rope to the rafter with Mom and Daddy none the wiser. Our parents thought they were rearing dainty little girls, but they were actually raising daredevil monkeys.

Jo and June in swings hung from the wheat house roof. Circa 1940.

27

If we didn't want to utilize the ladder, we could climb to the loft using our toes to grab hold of protruding nail heads.

We liked to climb up the ladder to the keyhole and sing at the top of our voices. Many of our selections were hymns sung at church and school. You could see forever from up there. When our arms got tired of hanging on, we'd climb back down.

Angels must have heard and looked after us as we actually survived these adventures at great heights.

One time when Jo and June walked back toward the house, Mom, angry and red-faced, was storming towards them. The cows had gotten out and Mom had called and called for them to come help her. They were singing so loudly they hadn't heard her. It was really

Babies with babies, June and Jo. Circa 1941.

unfortunate, but they both got a switching.

Mom was born in the wheat house, which was where Grandma and Grandpa lived until the new house under construction was finished.. After its completion, the wheat house was partitioned into four areas - two for wheat, one for barley and the other for oats. Seasonally corn was kept there as well. Segments of wheat were taken to the mill to be ground into flour.

Depending on the depth of the grain stored there; it was easy to get in and out of the sections. When it was nearly empty and the grain was shallow, I had to struggle to get back out. While it was full, we would bury ourselves in it.

The barn and wheat house offered excitement and adventure. However, eventually we were just three bored farm girls. When it was evening and time for the cows to return to the barn, we would take off our britches and position ourselves on two-by-fours in the over-hanging eave above the path the cows used. As they passed below, we'd try to pee between the cow's eyes. We stored as much ammunition as humanly possible and got fairly good at it. Another little little thing our parents never knew.

June, Judy and Jo on the farm. Circa 1948.

THE FARM HOUSE
Bollinger County, Missouri

There was an extra room in the farmhouse for a hired man but after Daddy moved to the farm he pretty much became that person. That room eventually was given over to Jo and June for a bedroom. Mom painted it and moved empty orange crates in. The orange crates were set on end and formed cubbies for their socks and underwear. She arranged cloth on strings to cover the clothing inside the orange crates and sewed curtains for the windows. A broom handle angled high against the wall served as a clothes rod for dresses and that area was curtained off as well.

Daddy had followed Mom to the farm and worked with Grandpa Looney from May to February 1938 when Grandpa passed away from stomach cancer. Daddy went out in the woods listening to hounds chase coons and sat on a cold tree trunk. The chill came up his backbone into his lungs causing pneumonia. Three times the pneumonia returned; it kept passing from one lobe to the other. Grandpa Looney was dying at the same time. Dr. Estes came and treated them both daily.

Daddy was put to bed in an unheated room where he sweated through the mattress. There was always a puddle beneath his bed that had to be mopped up several times each a day.

Mom would go to the barn to take care of the mules, milk the cows and feed the chickens, then back to the house to help care for the men. The house would fill with neighbors at night, some who stayed to sit with the sick men. Grandma Linebarger came and stayed two weeks to help.

Aunt Oma and Uncle Lloyd took year-old June home with them, not knowing she'd been exposed to chicken pox. They kept her until everyone recovered. They discovered they liked having a baby around, and about a year later, my cousin Donnie Brooks was born.

Previously, Mom was working in the kitchen one day and heard the living room bureau drawer close. She immediately recognized from the sound that the drawer was the one that held a pistol. She caught  up with Grandpa Looney as he was heading out the screened door onto the porch. She pulled him back into the house where they talked and talked. He was in extreme pain and wanted it to stop. Mom pleaded with him and the conversation ended with both of them lying across the bed crying. He passed away soon after.

Daddy's bedroom in Jackson had a picture of a Guardian Angel watching over two children as they play near a stream. It had been cut from a calendar and framed long before I was born. It had hung in the cold room on the farm where Daddy lay sick. He said he looked toward it each morning. If he saw it hanging there, he knew he had survived the night. It hangs near my bed now.

THE KITCHEN
The Heart of the Home

A cut-glass vase sat in the middle of the oilcloth covered kitchen table, where silverware was kept. Everyone took the pieces they needed, and after washing and drying, the silverware was dropped back into the vase.

The water bucket was on a table near the stove. It was filled from the cistern each morning and a drinking ladle hung from the rim.

Grandma's baking soda container, a small eared-bowl (it had little finger grips on either side), white with red flowers on it, stood nearby. There was a tiny spoon inside that held the exact amount of soda Grandma needed to make biscuits each morning.

After serving a substantial meal, like Sunday dinner, bowls or platters containing cooked items remained on the table. A large piece of white cloth was spread over it all to keep flies off the food, as we had no window screens. It was convenient for lifting the cloth edge and slipping out a biscuit or chicken leg between meals.

The utilitarian white metal cabinet in the kitchen had shelves for glasses and plates on the upper level behind glass-paned doors. The lower level had a large flour bin, which would hold copious amounts of milled or purchased flour. There was also a slide-out work board. The dinged and dented metal dishpan was placed on the cabinet for

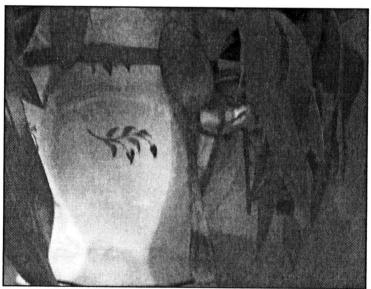

Grandma's baking soda jar with spoon. Photo 2016.

washing dishes, which were replaced on the shelves above after they were dried. The cabinet became a convenient storage space in the basement after we moved to Jackson, and the dishpan became a receptacle for garden vegetables waiting for processing.

When Daddy built the kitchen in Jackson, he, of course, included a flour bin and a slide-out work board. When doing homework, I would pull out the work board, which fit perfectly on the arms of the great chair Daddy had built for Grandma Linebarger. No matter how carefully I cleaned the board, my homework papers always had a residue of flour.

The cream separator lived next to the cabinet. Milking the cows was a twice-a-day chore. Sloshing buckets of fresh milk were carried to the house and emptied into the separator. The centrifugal force generated by cranking the devise separated the cream out of the whole milk. The cream was transported to town twice a week for sale, less a sufficient amount retained to make butter. To make the butter, the paddles were lowered into the cream inside the butter churn and we girls took turns cranking it.

Grandma Looney next to the farmhouse. Circa 1940.

After Mom had determined the texture of the butter was satisfactory, she'd squeeze any remaining fluid from the rich mound (resulting in buttermilk) and place it into a mold. One mold had an indented rose design, which would transfer to the soft butter. Milk warmed over a low flame until it curdled resulted in cottage cheese.

The big heat stove in the kitchen wasn't used during the hot months but clothing still had to be ironed. Unable to heat the irons the usual way, Mom used the kerosene iron in the summer. The iron was filled with kerosene and a handle was used to pump air into the iron. Then a flaming match was applied. In Mom's case, the iron would not light. She would take it apart, clean it, and go through the entire operation again. The iron would not light. Again, she disassembled the iron and cleaned it. The iron would not light. At that point, Mom would walk outside near the cistern and hurl the iron as far as she could into the yard. Then she'd walk out and retrieve it, put a lit match to it and the iron would work.

A shelf inside the flue box was just the right height to sit on while cranking the churn. Each stove had a flue box that had shelves built-in adjacent the stove flue, which ran all the way up to the roof.

Additionally, a small portable stove would be set up in Mom's bedroom and attached to the flue when she had a baby.

Several years before my birth, a man came to the farm and asked Mom for some used gunnysacks.

Silverware vase. Photo 2016.

The empty sacks were stored on top of a rafter in the wheat house. Mom got up on a ladder to get some down for him and strained herself resulting in a miscarriage. Daddy always said that baby would have been his boy.

One particular Friday, we went to an Eastern Star meeting with Mom. When we got home, Daddy said Santa Claus had visited while we were away. Even though his poker-playing cronies were there, he got down on one knee on the kitchen floor and opened a cabinet door to show me how Santa had knocked to deliver our presents.

Magically, a doll buggy appeared. It was wonderful! Jo and June got bicycles. It was cold and dark outside, but nothing would do but they had to ride them. June promptly ran into the side of the house and dented her fender, forever marking that bike as hers. Thereafter, the cats on the farm got lots of rides in the doll buggy, whether they wanted it or not.

BEDROOMS

Each bedroom had a chamber pot, or slop pot, depending on what each family called it. It was used as a toilet during the night, or forbidding weather, when a trip to the outhouse was unthinkable.

Once we had drinking straws. It was very exciting! However, as Mom passed food dishes back and forth her hand brushed a rigid straw and overturned a glass of milk. The third time that happened, Mom grabbed the straws out of the glasses and threw them outside through the open window. I found that
interesting as Mom never let her irritation show. From then on, our only straws were green onion stems. Still kind of fun, but it made the milk taste funny.

Mom would make Kool-Aid for us and put some into a baby bottle. Jo, June and I would fight to get to be the nursing baby. We would roll around on the linoleum kitchen floor sucking the bottle until she shooed us out. Sometimes I pretended I was a horse and grazed Cheerios from the seats of the kitchen chairs were I had sprinkled them.

Along with their bed, Mom and Daddy's bedroom included my baby bed and a pump organ with an unusual history. Grandpa Looney gave Mom a runt pig that was not getting enough milk to tend when she was a girl. She had a puppy, so she raised the pig and the puppy in a pen together. She sold the grown pig for twenty dollars and bought the pump organ from Grandpa Looney's cousin, Oran. It was like a church organ with a large adjustable mirror on top. A church organist would use the mirror to watch activity in the rear of the sanctuary to know what to play for the pastor, the choir or a bride to enter the center aisle.

After moving to Jackson, we discovered the large mirror for the top of the organ was missing. It was removed for an unknown reason, and probably stacked behind a bale of hay in the barn. Farmers lost many things that way, putting an item away where it was protected and then forgotten - especially truck tailgates.

I liked to sit on the organ stool and press the keys while pedaling like crazy. Often, something would brush the back of my legs

Mom with her calf. Circa 1925

Grandma Linebarger, Jo, and June on Mom's lap at the farm. Circa 1939.

and I'd swipe it away, again and again. Jo and June were hiding beneath my bed using a chicken feather to tickle my legs.

In Jackson, playing with the neighborhood kids, I often held down the bass keys to simulate an airplane engine. I was the pilot, and depending on how I pedaled, we were a fighter or passenger plane, crashing or not, dependent on how my legs held out.

We regularly received catalogues from Sears-Roebuck and Montgomery Ward on the farm. Grandma Looney used expired books to paste poems in that she'd clipped from the newspaper. I recall reading a number of Uncle Lloyd Brooks' poems.

I cut out catalogue models that I used as paper dolls. If I took Jo or June's turn drying dishes, one of them might play with me for a little while. Eventually, the outdated books found their way to the outhouse where they served as toilet paper.

*Jo with a view of the barn
behind her.
Circa 1939*

 # OUTSIDE AND GARDEN

The black iron cauldron located in an area near the garden was for boiling clothes clean. It held six to eight gallons of water. After it was filled, kindling beneath was ignited to heat the wash water. Doing laundry for six people was quite a chore. In the winter, Mom would have to wash indoors. She said her arms would near give out from wringing clothes. She hung the wet items in the attic, being careful not to slip off the rafter onto the lathe floor. If she had, she would've crashed into the room below.

The farmhouse roof was metal. During a rain, the water beat down on the metal, ran into the gutters and down a central downspout. The sound of the pattering rain was like lullaby and made for great sleeping. After about fifteen minutes, the roof was washed clean. A lever in a pipe connected to the downspout could then be opened and the water was redirected into the cistern. A hand-pump lifted the water to the surface to be collected in a bucket for drinking, cooking and washing. The cistern was deep so even in summer it was possible to get a refreshing drink of water.

One night on the farm, I woke up thirsty and went to the kitchen where the water bucket set on a table. I began to peck on it with my index finger nail while I sucked the thumb on the opposite hand.

Grandma wore a hearing aid that must have weighted three pounds, which she took off at night. Somehow, half-deaf as she was, she heard that pecking and got up to get me a dipper of water from the bucket.

During the summer, Grandma would sometimes go to the garden with a paring knife and set down in the dirt. She would peel garlic bulbs and eat the slices she cut off with the knife. It was the only time she'd do that.

In the 1930's, the county put in a new highway. The road had curved between the old garage and the hen house, passing by the edge of the barn lot. The new highway was constructed from Jessie Hartle's place to Henry Seabaugh's farm just north of ours. It eliminated a very large curve but cut through a section of the farm, isolating an entire field. Now the back of the house faced the new highway while the front of the house faced the woods and outbuildings. That curve had been home to the largest circumference Beech tree in the county. It was sacrificed in the name of progress.

Grandma Looney next to the cistern. The gutter drain pipe is just visible to the right of her shoulder. Circa 1936.

We had a rabbit hutch behind the house with a large crawl space beneath it. Grandma Looney's prescriptions were dispensed in heavy brown glass bottles with metal screw-on caps. We would play drug store beneath the rabbit hutch. There was nearly always a rain puddle under there that we'd use to fill the empty bottles and there

The end of two chicken hawks, June and Jo. Circa 1944.

were plenty of timbers to stack them on to display our inventory. Thank goodness Jo and June never decided to medicate me.

My family farmed corn, wheat, oats, hay and clover. The mules stayed in the barnyard and did team work. One died and the other was sold. Then they bought a team of horses, Toots and Johnny, who had a gray colt, Smokey Joe. Mom said we kids had made the colt a pet and ruined him for work. They couldn't get him to do anything at all.

Sufficient chickens were raised in the fall to be able to sell the excess that was not needed. Someone gave Mom some rabbits that she also raised and sold.

The orchard was a great place to play because a snack was usually hanging from a nearby tree. Persimmons were wonderful to eat pulled straight from the branch, still warm from the sun. However, it was necessary to have the patience to wait until after the first frost, which would sweeten and soften the fruit; otherwise, it was hard and bitter.

Rusty Coats brand apple trees grew in the orchard, as well as pears and peaches. In early spring, we picked wild onions in the woods.

We visited Uncle Frank, who had pecan trees. In addition to an abundant crop, our walnut tree always had a swing on it. Hickory nuts were gathered on our side of the orchard fence, the other side the hogs got. Around age four, I was on the walnut tree swing holding a puppy. I don't know what happened, but I woke up on the ground, minus the puppy.

The cows were driven across the highway to graze in the newly isolated field, a chore that required at least two people. The gate had to be opened, traffic monitored and any wandering cows herded in. There was no water source there, so the cows had to be fetched back every night. Eventually, they planted corn in that field.

There was a gooseberry bush near the path to the barn. We would often snuggle in beneath it, hidden from the casual glance, and feast on the berries.

We often walked through the fields to neighbor's houses. Mom always cautioned us to watch out if a sow had recent piglets. The sow would be a vigilant defender of her young. We made large circles around them.

The fruit orchard was separated from the alfalfa field by a wire fence. One day Grandma decided to

View of what was originally the front of the farmhouse.

41

clean up the orchard by burning all the fallen limbs and sticks lit-tering the ground. Shortly after lighting the bundle of sticks she'd gathered, the flames got out of control and the field caught fire.

A very pissed Mom and Daddy ran to the orchard with five-gallon buckets full of water. They dowsed gunnysacks in the buckets and beat the flames back with them. By the time it was out, a third of the field was gone. Daddy was so angry he refused to speak to Grand-ma. Finally that evening, Grandma apologized - a first. Daddy said, "If you want to burn something again, just let us know and we'll help you."

Lightning rods were on the house, barn and grain shed. Cables were buried about eighteen inches in the ground. If lightning struck and hit the rod, the charge would follow the cables into the ground. During lightning storms, we'd hide under the kitchen table. If light-ning struck, the whole house would shake.

Cousin Buck Drum and Mom, Cape Girardeau, circa 1932.

Jo on the front porch. The John Doggett house in the background. Jackson, circa 1955.

Jo in Mom's arms and Daddy holding June. Circa 1939.

I am from lying across the bed reading LITTLE HOUSE ON THE PRAIRIE *aloud to Mom while she worked at the bedroom sewing machine.*

When Mom moved to Cape to help Aunt Grace raise her three children, she would crochet designed squares at night. Grandma Looney was doing the same design on the farm. When Mom returned home for a weekend, they would crochet the squares together. This eventually resulted in a crocheted piece that could serve as a full bedspread or tablecloth for a large table. It looked fantastic with a colored cloth beneath it.

My mother's hands were never idle.

One night she tatted (made lace) all evening. When she was ready for bed she tossed a lace strip about eighteen inches long onto the ottoman she and Daddy shared for their feet. Daddy picked it up and scolded her for toiling so long on something she could've bought for a dime. She considered his opinion and quit tatting.

For years, Mom had made party dresses for the daughters of well-off mothers in Jackson and decorated them with her tatted lace. They were one-of-a-kind beauties and Mom usually smocked the bodice. The skirt was made out of taffeta and net, which could scratch the tender skin of little girls. So Mom bound the seams with double-fold bias tape that enclosed the offending edges inside a snug cotton cocoon. Thereafter, she applied store-bought lace. The usual price for one of these laborious dresses was $2.75.

Most flour, sugar and salt came in cloth sacks, which were saved for numerous functions such as our drawers (underwear), slips, dishtowels, aprons, and curtains. I was embarrassed in sixth grade during Play Day (a multi-grade sporting event) when the teacher asked a girl named Connie, who'd already competed, to change clothes with me (I was wearing a dress). Connie's jeans and matching shirt were heavenly cute but she donned my flour-sack dress and slip without complaint. Connie was always a class act.

Mom and I would go to Cape and walk all three blocks of downtown, drifting by J.C. Penney's, Sears and Roebuck's and Montgomery Ward. As we window-shopped, Mom would ask if I like this or if I liked that. Then we'd go back to Penney's where she'd buy remnants of fabric, and if I was lucky, twenty cents worth of chocolate-covered peanuts. Over the next few days, she sewed garments very similar to those in the store windows, only better. A gray wool skirt would have not one but six kick-pleats across the back with an epaulet over the top of them to cover the seam. Then she'd make a corresponding collar and cuffs for the sweater I'd wear with it.

As I grew older and more capable, the only way Mom would sew for me was if I did enough chores for her to have the time. That meant making all the beds, washing breakfast dishes and dry-mopping hardwood and linoleum floors before she got home from work. The sewing machine was in the corner of her bedroom and I often lay across the bed and kept her company. Then I began to read books to her. What joy, to read a passage I thought was funny and hear her laughter join mine! Wealth beyond belief! She liked to "chew my ears" (nuzzle my neck) and would often jump on the bed with me to do that very thing.

The first store-bought dress I ever had was for the ceremony the year I was a Jackson High School senior class Carnival queen candidate. It was blue gown, strapless, ruffle after ruffle floor-length and gorgeous. There was a parade through town in the afternoon. I sat on the back of a white convertible wearing a knee-length strapless red formal I'd borrowed from Donna Byrd. I carried a dozen red roses, a surprise gift from my boyfriend. Later I was schooled on how to perform a deep curtsy and could hardly walk by that night for the sore leg muscles. My campaign manager, Larry Decker, very handsome in dark trousers and a white jacket, escorted me. Unfortunately, I lost, but anyone would have been a knock-out in that dress.

Jo worked at the hosiery mill after high school, which made stockings. After buying a pair of panty hose, it was prudent to make

*Senior Carnival Queen candidate with my campaign manager, Larry
Decker, driving. Jackson, 1961.*

them them wet, put them in a plastic bag and freeze. Somehow that
process made the fiber stronger.

When Jo began to earn money, she started buying some lovely
store-bought clothes. Rather than hang them in the closet in her
room, she just carefully laid them on the steps going upstairs. I really liked them, they were so pretty, especially the sweaters. So - one
day I tried them on and they fit.

I had a great time for several months. I left after Jo in the morning, wearing her clothes, and arrived back home before she did in
the afternoon, when I carefully replaced the clothes. She puzzled a
long time over why they weren't clean, especially her sweaters. She
finally figured it out and I was warned to exclusively wear my own
wardrobe.

There just wasn't anything my mother couldn't do with a needle
and thread. She had all the scrap shoe factory velvet at her disposal
(that's discussed later, too), so one year she made each daughter,
son-in-law and grandchild a robe. She'd finish one, hold it up and
say "that should fit so-and-so." There was no pattern, just the deci-

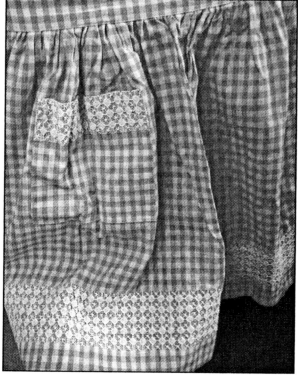

Gingham apron with crochet thread lace-like insert.
Circa 1966.

sion to make the next one shorter or longer. I've never attempted to multiply how many button holes she sewed that Christmas.

The same was true the year she made us girls gingham aprons. She made numerous rows of design with crochet thread that made it look like a lace insert. I still have mine.

When I returned as a mother with my kids to visit, we were always eager to see what the new craft would be. Once it was yarn twisted over floral wire to form roses. It became a tradition that after Thanksgiving dinner, we'd all do a craft.

Once we put Styrofoam cups on a baking sheet in a hot oven where they shrunk and melted into unique shapes. We painted them and decorated them as small hats. We added ribbons around the crown, feathers, jewels, beads, whatever embellishments looked best. My son, Jeff, made one and put it on Jo's statue of an American

Flannel lined lap robe. Photo 2016.

eagle. The eagle still wears it.

For one session, Mom said she needed fifty small thank you gifts for her going-out-of-office as Worthy Matron of the Eastern Star banquet. (Mom got her fifty-year membership pin a year or so before she passed away.) We made boxes out of used greeting cards, filled them with M&M candies and tied them closed with gold elastic cord. They were enthusiastically received.

In the Eastern Star, Mom was usually an officer, which necessitated a formal gown. By that time, she and Daddy had raised garage-sale shopping to an art form. They bought anything polyester and Mom bought every wedding gown she came across. She used the satin skirts and trains for her Eastern Star dresses and made stoles or jackets from lace.

My folks took home the polyester garments, laundered them, and then began the arduous task of dismantling them. Buttons were removed and saved in a box, zippers were taken out and saved in another box, seams were ripped open and pieces pressed flat. Daddy had cut square sheet-metal patterns that measured four, three or two inches. He cut the four-inch squares first with the whole garment, then worked to snip as many three-inch squares out of the scraps, and finished with the two-inch ones.

When Daddy had amassed sufficient piles of square, Mom began to lay them into designs and sew them together into quilts. Some of the quilts were lined with flannel. If you fell asleep beneath one of them, you awoke sweating and thirsty. They wanted to make a quilt for my king-sized bed. It finished at nine feet by nine feet and required them both to hold it while Mom sewed. I valued it as a true labor of love.

Years after I was married and was a mother myself, I would occasionally get a package from Mom with a dress or two inside. If it happened to be a sundress, a small tab with a snap at the opposite end was sewn beneath the shoulder seam. The idea was to pass the tab under my bra strap and snap it into place. That was in the days when a lady didn't want her bra straps to show, pre-Madonna. After a pressing, the new dresses were ready to wear, always a perfect fit.

Lewis and Clark Expedition plaque at Trail of Tears Park, Cape Girardeau.
Photo 2016.

50

Jo and June. Circa 1940.

June, Judy and Jo.

Judy in Jackson. Mable and Wes Henderson home in the background. Circa 1953.

I am from Saturday afternoon dime double-features and five-cent ice cream cones.

Riding the fifteen miles to Jackson on a Saturday was a highly anticipated event. Jo, June and I were dropped at the Jackson Theater for the matinee, which was usually a western movie. My weekly allowance was twenty-five-cents (at the time, I didn't really know how much money that was) and the fee for admission was a dime. We never bought a concession item. Popcorn was the only thing offered, and Mom made that at home in a large black cast-iron skillet.

Selection of just the right seat was a much enjoyed process; I usually sat between Jo and June. It wasn't so much they wanted to protect me as it was to make sure no one mistreated me, other than them.

The excitement of sitting in the dark and watching a story unfold was rampant among the children in attendance. The theater had a wide middle section of probably twenty seats to a row with an aisle on both sides. Adjacent each aisle was another section of perhaps ten seats. Public smoking was permitted at that time and those who indulged usually sat in the back row where the seats had built-in ashtrays.

African-American children took the balcony. They were not encouraged to sit there but usually did. If white children were up there, you could expect them to occasionally pelt you with popcorn.

Eventually, the house lights would fade as the first reel called "News of the World" began. The logo was an airplane circling a globe. It was incredibly boring to a child eager for a rip-roarin' shoot 'em up movie.

Then a serial (a movie done in sequential segments) played that was exciting beyond words. The ending was always a cliffhanger, leaving you anxious for the damsel in distress tied to the railroad tracks, or the white-hatted hero mounted on his faithful steed leaping from a cliff to save her.

Next was a hilarious Warner Brothers, Disney or Walter Lantz cartoon. They featured Tom and Jerry, Woody Woodpecker, Mickey Mouse, Goofy, Felix the Cat, Pepe Le Pew and more, all great stuff!

Then the western began. I saw a few Ken Maynard movies but was too young to have ever seen Buster Crabbe or Tom Mix, although I knew Tom's horse was named Tony. Roy Rogers and Gene Autry were the favorites of my day. Rex Allen, Tim Holt, Hopalong Cassidy, Randolph Scott, Lash LaRue, Judy Canova, The Lone Ranger,

The Jackson (Cape Girardeau County) Courthouse.
The Palace Movie Theater was located at the opposite
end of the street. Photo 2016.

and Wild Bill Hickok each dropped by once in a while. Sidekicks Pat Brady, Smiley Burnette, Jingles, Chico, Bullet, Dale Evans, or Gabby Hayes would accompany their starring partner.

On Sunday mornings we three would pile into bed with Mom and Daddy. Daddy would start asking trivia questions: What is the name of Roy Rogers horse? Trigger? Gene Autry's horse? Champion. What is the name Pat Brady's jeep? Nelly Bell. I was good at remembering. It began a lifetime of retaining facts that would never

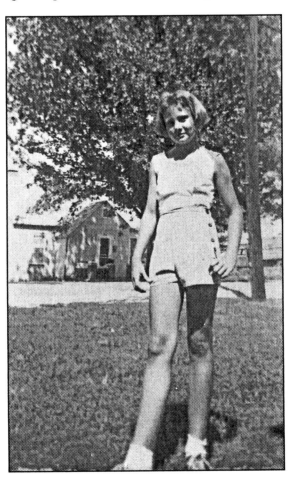

Judy in Jackson. Talley house visible across the street. Circa 1954.

55

Grandpa Linebarger's in Cape. Me, and Cousin James Green in front, with June, Jo and Cousin Donnie Brooks in back. Circa 1948.

make me one-cent as a result of that knowledge.

Mom and Daddy never attended the matinees. But my sister Jo told me that on the farm they would sometimes go to bed at night with their clothes on. They would quietly wait for the house to fall asleep. Then they'd creep out of bed, grab their shoes and head for the car. Often as Daddy backed the car out and the headlights swept the yard, they'd spot me in my pajamas standing by the cistern waving bye-bye. Rather than risk putting me back into bed and waking everyone up, Mom would whisk me into the car with them and take me along to the movies.

Saturday night we might listen to Gene Autry on the battery-operated radio. He would introduce his show by saying he was at his ranch in California. I didn't know how far away that was, but I was very impressed that I'd just watched him in Jackson that afternoon and was already home.

It was years later that western feature-length dramas with stars the likes of John Wayne, Clint Eastwood, Steve McQueen and Gary Cooper were filmed. The ones we enjoyed were matinee idols, not movie stars.

After hours in the dark theater, we'd stumble out into the sunlight

Judy and Cousin James Green. Cape Girardeau, circa 1948.

and make our way down Main Street to Roloff's Drug Store. At that time, to me, it was the equivalent of a Sam's Club with its many aisles choked full of merchandise. I was forbidden to ever touch anything in there. Five cents would pay for a double dip of ice cream on a specially shaped double sugar cone. I usually got chocolate and chocolate. (Don't mess with perfection.)

When we returned to the street, we would spot the family car at the curb waiting for us. In the two hours we were in the movie, Mom and Daddy would've carried out five or six in-town errands at the grocery store, feed store, hardware, drug store, or just visited friends.

There was a discrepancy in my finances. Ten cents for the show and five cents for ice cream doesn't add up to my twenty-five-cents-a-week allowance. I was much older when one day my mother placed a quarter in my hand.

"Here's your allowance," Mom said.

I was astounded! I asked, "Do I get this much money?"

Mom said, "You always have."

That's when I figured out that apparently Jo and June had been splitting my other ten cents each week. Sisters!

Jo – 12, June – 11 and Judy – 5 – on the farm, 1948.

I am from classroom prayer, **Pledge of Allegiance,** *marching band, and home economics class.*

The country school day began with the Pledge of Allegiance followed by the Morning Prayer. We rose from our desks, faced the U.S. flag in the corner, placed our right hands over our hearts, and recited the Pledge together. Following the Pledge, our teacher, Miss Mildred Statler, led us in prayer. Then she played the piano near the side window while we sang hymns. She chose the first two songs; we took turns requesting the final hymn. My favorite was "I Shall Not Be Moved", *like a tree that's standing by the water, I shall not be moved.* We could really belt out the chorus.

The desks were constructed to accommodate two students each on a bench-like seat. The top surface had an obsolete circular opening cut into it that would have provided access to a bottle of ink at one time. (A student dipped the pen nib into the ink to transfer it to paper. There were old-time stories that boys would dip the end of the braided hair of the girl sitting in front of them into the ink well for sport.) A shelf beneath was for books and student supply storage.

An enormous coal stove occupied most of the rear corner. In winter, the desks were repositioned to a semi-circle near it for warmth. Warning: if you drop your cherished wad of bubble gum that you've saved for days and it hits a cinder that has popped out of the stove, it's impossible to remove all parts of said cinder. Your bubble gum will forever "crunch."

Coat racks were in the opposite corner along with a water bucket. The front wall was covered with blackboards and maps. A bench was positioned beneath the window opposite the one by the piano, to the left of Miss Mildred's desk.

We were called up front to recite lessons by grade. There were four of us in the second grade; we were the largest group of the thirteen

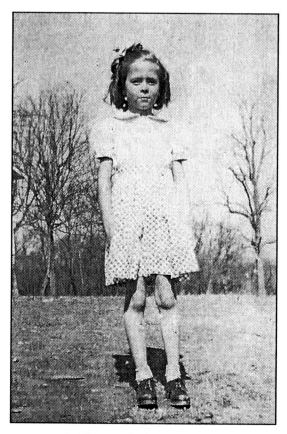

Jo Ellen on the farm, 1945.

students. While others recited, we worked on assignments at our desks and listened to their responses to Miss Mildred's questions. I always sat with one sister or another, and when she left to recite, I would often lie down on the seat and take a nap.

There were spelling or geography bees in which we all participated. Once when I was sitting at a desk with June, the game was Name State Capitols. I asked her if one of the states was like her name; she was Carolyn June. It took a second to register and then her hand shot up for North and South Carolina, followed by the Dakotas. Jo Ellen didn't have any states that contained part of her name.

There were two outhouses, (mandatory that each school have one

Carolyn June on the farm, 1945.

for boys and one for girls). Often after I'd returned from "outside," Jo would motion me over and pull up the zipper on my britches.

Swings were beneath several trees on the property, which was nearly surrounded by woods. At noon we broke off in groups to eat our lunch and play. Occasionally, a baseball game was organized with everyone on a team, even Miss Mildred. I'd never seen a woman's bosom do the things hers did when she ran the bases. My "Easy Out" nickname was well-deserved and remained with me all my life since my athletic skills never developed. I watched and tried to improve, I even made it to third by stealing bases once. About that time, the runners already on second and third started loud protests. I'd missed a key rule that stated the base must be unoccupied when

Judith Grace on the farm, 1945.

The Linebarger Girls on the farm in 1945.

Third grade, age 9

attempting to steal. Rats! I'd nearly made home. We had one baseball, one bat and one basketball which were shared without fuss. Lunch and recess ended when Miss Mildred rang her brass hand bell.

June was giving a book report on *Peter Pan* one afternoon, looking out the window while she talked. I heard her say that a car had stopped on the road near the swings, then a person got out and grabbed our basketball. The person jumped back into the car and sped off. Miss Mildred didn't even look up. June finished and repeated the theft to Miss Mildred. She scolded June for not saying anything (like we were going to run outside and catch the car). The students backed June up but the ball was long gone. I even took better care of my "horse" stick after that happened. .

Judy, June and Jo on the farm. Circa 1946.

63

*Judy, fourth grade, age 10, wearing Jackson High
Band Uniform. Circa 1953.*

I am from classroom prayer, Pledge of Allegiance, marching band, and home economics class.

The Jackson High School band played a concert in the grade school auditorium when I was nine. The final piece of the program was Stars and Stripes Forever by Sousa. A senior named Madge Roloff played the thrilling piccolo part that flits and flies with the agility of a hummingbird above the rest of the instruments.

After the concert, Leroy Mason, the band director, invited the elementary student body to consider joining the band by taking music lessons. When Mr. Mason said that eventually we could play those same instruments we just heard - I immediately volunteered, which was a shock. As a third grader, I never opened my mouth. And just as quickly, I was informed that I had to learn to play the flute before I could play the piccolo.

A young girl in a nearby community had developed tuberculosis and her family sold Mom her flute for fifty dollars. It was a huge investment for my folks to make in me. It apparently never occurred to any of us just how contagious TB was and that I could get sick using it. We did, of course, wipe it off with a cloth.

Mom sewed a carrier for the flute case and I began lessons that summer. There were four of us in the class. Mr. Mason sat behind us on the bandstand in the music room with his baton in hand. When he tapped my shoulder with the tip of the baton and said, "Judy, count that measure," I started crying. I was terrified of him.

In fourth grade, Mr. Mason came to our classroom and requested the teacher permit the four flute players to practice with the marching band for an hour first thing every morning. He needed bodies, not musicians. Incredibly, the teacher and grade school principal agreed to the arrangement.

Mr. Mason had developed what was then an entirely new technique for performance. A segment of the band members would form a large square. As we marched down the football field, the remaining members within the square would spell out the letters in "J-A-C-K-S-O-N" (we were the Jackson Indians). On the return trip up the field, we spelled "I-N-D-I-A-N-S." It was very impressive and widely copied.

I learned to read the formation charts Mr. Mason handed out each week, and he always kept me beside the same baritone horn player, Chad. No matter where Chad went during practice, I was two steps behind, each step measuring twenty-two and one-half inches. If he would've gone into the boys' bathroom, I'd have stood outside the door marching in place until he exited.

It could've mattered less whether or not I could play the music. It was impossible to hear my flute above the percussion and brass on a football field.

The Municipal Bandstand situated on the Courthouse lawn. Photo 2016.

I was outfitted with a uniform that included a red jacket with gold braid through an epaulet, black trouser with a red stripe down the side seam, black leather Sam Brown belt, policeman-like hat and white spats. From the age of ten until seventeen when I graduated, I was in the marching band. During football season, we played and marched for every game, at home and away. From day one, I was treated as a short but equal member.

My glamorous friend, Sharon, became the majorette for the band in high school. She wore a beaded white leather fringed dress and an Indian headdress. She carried a long baton and used it to accent the beat as she led the band.

Band practice was always the first thing on school mornings. We girls threw our vanity to the wind and put curlers in our hair before going outside. Otherwise, we were cursed with limp hair all day, devoid of body from the moisture in the air and dew on the ground.

When I started seventh grade at age twelve, I became part of the Jackson High School Music Band. From tenth grade on, I was also part of the concert band, which required auditions. The audition piece was the "chase" music used in movie cartoons - very fast and difficult, hitting C above high C. I practiced often, propping the music on the organ's holder in the living room. Often I would catch a glimpse of Mom standing in the door from the kitchen, drying her hands with a dishtowel and listening.

The wooden three-tiered bandstand on the football field was positioned about a foot away from the cement wall of the stadium. Mr. Mason watched the practice from the topmost heights of the grandstand, and when angered, he descended the
steps in a rush, stepped from the stadium wall, hitting the top rail of the bandstand and thundered onto the field to chew someone out. I managed to avoid these tirades. I played the flute and followed Chad - I could do no wrong!

During the afternoon of one of the band festivals, Mr. Mason worked himself into a rage and came flying down from the highest tier. When he stepped for the top rail of the bandstand, he missed, and vanished from sight. We truly didn't know how to react; we all loved and feared him. That evening he conducted the program with his newly broken arm in a sling.

Nights were cold on the bandstand during the late autumn months. Mr. Mason smoked a pipe and I would watch the smoke form a halo around his head. Today when I smell that tobacco scent, I still get a warm feeling. A big finish to the school year was the band banquet. It felt very special to have something prepared for just the band members.

The mimeographed cover of the Band Banquet program.

It was amazing, but we actually found schools smaller than our own to go play concerts. We might ride a school bus for hours along gravel roads with overgrown tree branches whipping the windows to a tiny building where we'd set up and play. I think it was supposed to enlighten them, but mostly we played unfamiliar classical music.

Mr. Mason left our school and became conductor at Southeast Missouri State College in Cape Girardeau. When I went to band camp there during the summer of my junior year, he introduced me to his colleagues as one of his "Jackson babies."

Our next band director was Mr. Partridge. As we went out for morning practices we would sing the refrain "and a partridge in a pear tree" from *The Twelve Days of Christmas*, in what we considered high jest. One Thursday evening while he conducted the municipal band's weekly concert in the gazebo on the court house lawn, Mr. Partridge was arrested for armed robbery. He was still wearing his uniform when photographed by the local newspaper getting into the police cruiser. Two bank tellers in the concert audience, from different nearby towns, identified him as the man who had robbed them.

Mr. Partridge had a passel of his own children who were in band with us, poor guys. He'd been in heavy debt and after the robberies, paid off many bills in cash. He said the gun he used had never been loaded. When he was released a few years later, one of the city leaders fired a worker in order to give Mr. Partridge a job.

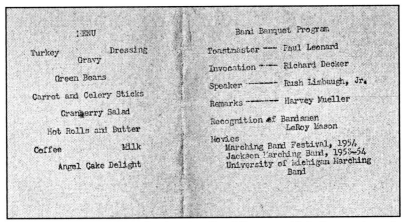

The menu and program for the 1955 Band Banquet. Note the guest speaker.

I really liked Mr. Carson, my last music director. I was first chair on the front row of flutes so when he'd get a phone call during a piece of music, he'd hand me the baton to conduct. It was wonderful! I have no idea where my shy self disappeared to, but I have a feeling that a small dose of musical knowledge is what gave me courage. I could instantly read the enormous pages that showed what each section of instruments was playing and could cue them with the baton to come on the correct beat.

Usually by ten o'clock at night, bedtime for most folks, our football games ended. If we won a home game, Mr. Carson would march us through town playing a rousing (no pun intended) tune.

On a double date one night after a football game and marching through town, we went to an abandoned farmhouse with a couple of football players. My girlfriend and I still had on our band uniforms. The pitch darkness made the house even spookier to explore and was great fun.

Several weeks later, during morning practice, Mr. Carson lifted up a uniform jacket that a farmer had found in his corn field. The number inside it identified it as mine. Mr. Carson and the farmer were wondering how it had ended up in the farmer's field. I was dumbfounded; I hadn't even missed it! I turned multiple shades of red as I blushingly tried to explain the innocence of that particular evening. Shaking his head from side to side, even the farmer didn't believe me.

I'm happy to say flute playing still runs in the family. My son played the flute until he started high school. In junior high, he was the only boy in a class with fourteen girls. My granddaughter, Racheal, went to the Berkeley School of Music in Boston with her flute. She's a music therapist in California now.

I never did get to play the piccolo, but I gave granddaughter Racheal one when she graduated high school.

I am from classroom prayer, Pledge of Allegiance, marching band, and **home economics class.**

My mother was thirty-three when I was born. I was fourteen when I took my first home economics class from Miss Roberta Ranney, who had also been my mother's home economics instructor. Miss Ranney was gray, bent and worn. Somewhere along the way, she'd lost her zest for teaching.

The Home Economics wing shared a building across the street from the high school. Our classes were about meal preparation, nutrition, sewing, ironing, grocery shopping, food preservation, etc.

The Future Farmers of America had class in the opposite wing. Their subjects were animal husbandry, soil enrichment, crop rotation, irrigation, and cultivation methods. Most were members of 4-H, an organization which stands for Head, Heart, Hands, and Health. Both the FFA and Home Economics had a club and elected officers. Pins were given for membership; the year I was Home Economics president, a tiny silver gavel was affixed to my pin.

The Music Department occupied the opposite side of the building. That area had practice rooms, the bandstand, instrument storage, and offices.

The Home Economics Department had four complete identical kitchens at one end. When we cooked breakfast, four or five students worked in each kitchen. A strip of bacon, an egg, a slice of toast and a glass of orange juice were prepared. Then it was divided among us and eaten; it was surprisingly unsatisfying.

After cleaning up, we wrote a report for Miss Ranney describing the process employed to prepare the scant meal, denoting the location of the spatula, the forks, the skillet, the toaster, etc. It was mind numbing.

The sewing classes were slightly more interesting. At home,

*Mom – about the time she would have taken
Home Economics.*

Mom had a Singer treadle (a foot pedal) sewing machine. If one made the mistake of starting to treadle with the needle in the down position, it would unthread itself. If one didn't immediately stop, the upper and bobbin threads would magically stitch themselves together into an impermeable knot. I got similar results with fishing line when I tried to cast a lure.

Miss Ranney wanted us to sew a pillowcase, a very elementary assignment. Sew straight seams, press in a hem, and stitch it all together. Mom was not about to go to town and buy a length of fabric for my project, she just cut me a section from a worn out bed sheet. My pillow case was enormous. I could have covered an easy chair. Thereafter, Miss Ranney provided the exact measurements for the finished product.

Eventually, we had to make a dress. Mom gave me a piece of fabric that was soft blue, pink and yellow squares. I cut out a sundress with a square-necked bodice and a gathered skirt. I'd done a fairly good job matching the squares to line up on the seams, but I'd trimmed them too severely. The weekend before it was due, I took my mess of a dress home and disassembled it. Mom helped me sew it back together by the Monday morning deadline. Miss Ranney drilled me about whether my mom had sewn it for me; I denied it to the end. She had merely supervised from the chair next to mine at the sewing machine.

In my junior year of high school, a man carried a microwave oven into our classroom. It was the size of a modern stove. He gave us quite a spiel about the wonders it could perform, but I was from Missouri – show me. The demonstrator put a fresh ear of popping corn into a brown paper bag, then put the bag into the microwave. We heard it begin to pop and could smell that wonderful aroma of fresh hot popcorn. It was incredible and took no time to prepare! He poured it into a bowl and held up the now naked corncob. We munched in wonder and speculated whether we'd ever be rich enough to own such a magical device.

Standing at a distance wearing a skeptical frown, Miss Ranney observed the demo while tapping her chin with her forefinger. I suspect she was thinking this new-fangled notion would never come to fruition. Her disapproval was apparent.

I mentioned the demonstration to a friend in Ohio. A microwave was also brought into his school. I wondered if sales personnel went to every high school in the early 1960's preparing a demographic eager to purchase the perfected microwave when it hit the market.

In Miss Ranney's defense, the microwave was probably the first new idea that had crossed the threshold of her classroom in decades.

I wonder what she'd make of the Cooking Channel.

Mom - a woman of her time. Circa 1928.

HORSE CRAZY

From the time I was a young girl I was horse crazy. I could be lying upside down in the back seat of the car and Mom would say, "There's a pretty horse over in that field." In a flash I was upright with my nose pressed against the car window.

I liked the size of a horse, its smell, the feel of its muscles contracting and releasing when I rode bareback. The sounds it made – a nicker of recognition, a whinny to a distant friend, a rumble of gratitude in its throat for an apple. I loved the shape of its nose, the "I'm-not-kidding" warning its ears signaled when they flattened

Mom is going to have a problem mounting that horse. On the farm, circa 1928. There was a side-saddle in the farm house attic. Mom said she had never used it; it belonged to Grandma Looney.

against its skull, and the velvety softness of its muzzle. I was drawn to them as surely as horseflies and gnats.

I disobeyed and often prayed for a horse – prayers were not supposed to be selfish. I had relentlessly supported the proposition that it would be quite convenient to stable a horse in our Jackson basement, where I would take care of it. My folks offered no encouragement whatsoever for that idea. It was like they weren't even listening.

After Grandma Looney passed away, I was moved from the day-bed in the living room to her bedroom. Her double-bed had an iron bedstead. The round top piece came up from both sides, arched toward the center, then arced again in the middle. The bottom piece was higher than the mattress but was flat across.

Mom playing around.

When longing for a mount, imagination is a necessity. A bed pillow thrown over the top arc of the bedstead and a belt from a robe wrapped around one of the forward frame spokes created a perfect horse, complete with bridle and saddle. Neighbor Ruth Ann Talley and I often spent the night racing against each other toward a distant finish line. We applied supple whips cut from Weeping Willow limbs to urge our steeds to greater speed. Her old plug never won against my sleek "head-of-the-bed" thoroughbred.

Around age seven, Mom's niece, Glendell, took me to St. Louis for a week to be company for her son Rex. She and her husband Stacey Gearing lived near a railroad track with rumbling trains that woke me in the wee hours of the morning. This was the flip side to utterly quiet nights on the farm. Rex was about four or five and as Stacey explained it, suffered from "bite-i-tious." As proof, he showed me the back of a new soft vinyl dinette chair that had a permanent impression of Rex's teeth in it. They had a friendly furry dog named Pudgy so I was happy enough.

While Rex took an afternoon nap, I played with two little girls next door. Behind their house was a small corral holding a large horse named Red Bird. The girls asked if I'd like to ride him and I said I sure would. Between the three of us, we managed to get the saddle and bridle on him. I was boosted into the saddle and the gate was opened.

It was early spring and as I later learned, Red Bird had been in a stable or that small corral all of the long, long winter. When the gate stopped moving, Red Bird's ears perked forward and the next second he exploded out of the corral into the immense open field next door.

Glen had just stepped out her back door to see what I was up to as I galloped by her on a red flash. I can still remember the sound of her frantic screams, "Judy, get off that horse this instant."

I lost and re-found the stirrups several times and wondered how to regain control of the bit that Red Bird had imprisoned between his teeth. I finally just hung on and let him run. It was thrilling!

Then, it was terrifying! I could see in the distance that the field ended adjacent a six-lane highway with cars whizzing by. There was no fence. I braced my feet in the stirrups and hauled back on the reins. Abruptly, he slowed. Red Bird had exhausted enough of his exuberance over being able to exercise that he allowed me to rein him back toward the barn.

I could see the girls, ever so small on the horizon, and Glen lying in the field. I didn't know then that she'd thrown up, numerous times, and her face was wet with tears. She was probably rehearsing the speech she'd give my parents explaining my death. We walked back toward them and as anticipated, when we reached Glen, she grabbed my arm and pulled me off Red Bird. She could hardly walk and I couldn't stop smiling. As a defense mechanism, I kept my head down so she wouldn't see the excited glee on my face.

Glen handed the reins to my friends and led me into the house.

Rex was still napping, so she gave me milk and a cookie and instructed me to stay in the kitchen while she took a shower. (She really needed one). Over supper, she and Stacey made me promise I'd never get on Red Bird again. They hadn't told me not to ride the neighbor's horse, so I wasn't punished. I vowed I would stay off Red Bird, but always kept an eye out for another opportunity, just in case. I don't know that Glen ever told mother about that little episode.

Following my adventure in St. Louis, life back in the country was mild. During fair weather when we walked from the farm to Jesse and Rainey's, June would neigh at the horses we saw along the way. Often the horses would neigh back, but once in a while, one would start running at us and scare us silly.

Cookie, the field horse, had been overworked and when Daddy got her. Jo and June were allowed to give her apples and nubs of corn. They could hang on her legs and neck, pull on her ears, anything they wanted to do but get on her back. When Daddy took her to plow a field, cutting that first square around the edges, Cookie would stumble and stagger. Once back to the beginning, Cookie would take one step toward the inside and plow a furrow as straight as any seeing horse. When released at the end of the workday, Cookie took herself back to the barn, hitting each open gate dead center.

On the morning of my twelfth birthday, I glanced out at the field located behind our house in Jackson and noticed a grazing black and white pony! I'd gotten a pony for my birthday! I was over the moon, excited, and incredulous. I ran to the kitchen and thanked Mom and Daddy, who appeared to be dumbfounded. They looked out the window of the sun room at the pony and apologized. They hadn't gotten me a pony. The pony was not for me. (Scream!) They got me a doll. (Scream!) My last doll. The family rule was no more dolls after the twelfth birthday.

The pony was for the step-grandchildren of Wilson Lewis, who one day would become my father-in-law. (He didn't give my children a damn pony!) Our yard abutted both the step-son's house and the pony's pasture, so the children crossed our far back yard to get to it. I observed their fun with bitter envy. Then I noticed that when

Capaha Park, Cape Girardeau. Circa 1953.

it was raining, they didn't ride Oreo. (I'd taken the liberty of giving him an appropriate name.) So that was when I played with him. I was never spotted stealing bareback rides through the pouring rain.

I think Mom must've felt sorry that I was so disappointed because she never scolded me for pilfering rides. When I came back home, she would just looked me up and down, soaking wet and reeking of horse and say, "Get to the basement for a shower and leave those clothes down there."

Joe Manning Mathews and I were born at the same hospital on the same day. His mother and mine shared a room. Every year from second to sixth grade, Joe and I were sent out of the classroom into the corridor. During our absence, our teacher would draw a birthday cake on the blackboard. When we were invited to return, our classmates would sing Happy Birthday.

Joe had a black and white horse named Partner. My jealousy flares to this day. Partner would stick his head through the kitchen window to beg for apple slices while Joe ate breakfast.

One Sunday afternoon at Capaha Park in Cape, I ran into my cousin Donnie sitting on a horse. Donnie knew about my passion for equine beings and promptly helped me into the saddle. The park had a large pond that I rode the horse around, reluctantly returning it to Donnie. In retrospect, Mom had suggested we go to Cape and then stopped at Capaha Park, something we'd never done. I suspect Donnie had alerted Mom that he would be there on a friend's horse.

In my mind, any horse that showed up in my neighborhood was fair game. So when someone put a horse in the pasture behind my friend's house, I devised a plan for riding it. First, I needed bait, so I took carrots from the refrigerator crisper and climbed the fence surrounding the field.

He was a handsome fellow and very tall. I fought the wasps with only a few stings to nab the bridle I discovered in a storage shed. He was docile about my putting it on and followed me quite willingly to a tree with a low branch. I positioned him carefully and climbed the tree. Then he shifted his weight and stepped to the side, moving him several feet too far from the limb. I had to climb back down the tree, walk him in a circle and position him again. The third time down the tree, a movement to the side caught my eye. Mom. She was standing at the fence watching me. She had a switch in her hand, and she was pissed.

I removed the bridle and carefully replaced it in the shed, got a few more stings, and secured the door. I dragged one foot as I walked to Mom and climbed the fence. From there to the house I danced. She used that switch on the back of my legs all the way home. Note to self – don't steal Mom's carrots for horse bait.

After I married, my husband's uncle invited us to visit his farm. My husband had a new .22 gauge rifle and wanted to shoot mistletoe out of the tree tops for Christmas decorations and I wanted to ride Tony, the horse that was stabled there. My husband helped me saddle and bridle Tony and went to stalk the woods. Tony and I left the barnyard at a slow walk onto a gravel road. Tony was immune to urgings for a quicker pace. Eventually, I turned Tony around, which was when he saw the barn roof. Suddenly, poke-along-Tony was galloping.

I tried to slow Tony down, but the bridle had been applied incorrectly and he wouldn't respond to the reins. About the same time, I noticed that I was no longer square on Tony's broad back. I was slightly aslant. As we continued heading for his pasture at a good bouncing speed, I slipped farther past his shoulder and sagged, in tiny jerks, toward the underside of his belly until I hit the gravel road.

The stirrups of the upside down saddle were dragging on the gravel. I tried to loosen the girth to re-align it, but Tony had puffed up his belly so it could not be adjusted. My husband's uncle arrived to see me standing in the middle of the road with his horse. Neither the saddle nor bridle was correctly applied. We were not invited back.

My last horseback ride was a gift from my daughter Kim. She was working in Oak Ridge, Tennessee and sent a gift certificate for a horseback ride through the Smokey Mountains for Mother's Day, but I had to go get it.

It was beautiful weather the morning we took the ride. My mount was Jake, a veteran of the trail. The guide cautioned us as we came to a stream not to let the horses drink from it. Jake and I had a tug-of-war trying to keep his mouth above the water. By the time we crossed behind the other horses, the opposite bank was slick with mud and Jake jostled me around climbing it.

The only sounds were from birds and insects as we walked through forested glens. When we came upon a family of grazing deer, they merely raised their heads and looked at us before returning to breakfast. They had no fear of people mounted on horses.

One side of the trail was a mountain; the other side was empty air. It was so narrow it made my stomach clutch to look over the edge, which was straight down for a very long way. I didn't think we could travel on the ledge without my leg touching the mountain, but we did. Occasionally, I tried to rein Jake nearer the mountain but he would not budge from the track he wanted to follow. I finally gave up, relaxed the reins and enjoyed my surroundings.

When we returned to the stables, the owner, I'll call him Sam, said that had Jake slept the entire route. I said I had also. Sam told us a story about the mountain roads and how dangerous they were. He was in his truck with his wife when they were rear-ended by a carload of teenagers. Sam asked, "Do you know what I did to those kids?" I feared what he'd say next. "I had them to my house for a steak dinner!" Sam's wife had been suffering from continual back pain for years with no relief. After the car rear-ended them, something was jarred back into place and her back pain became history.

We weren't in any hurry and Sam relished telling stories, so he told us a better one. A family from Iowa had vacationed together in Florida and was on their way back home. They asked if Sam would permit their blind teenaged son, (I'll call him Joe) to ride the trail. Sam assured them that the horse knew the way, so if the son could hang on there would be no problem.

All went well until they crossed the afore-mentioned stream and Joe's horse started up the muddied bank. The horse's hooves slipped and he fell to his knees. As the horse went down, he bounced Joe, who rolled right down the horse's neck smack onto his back on the muddy ground. Everyone stopped and brushed Joe off, who was unharmed, and joked about his riding skill. They got him back on his mount and finished the ride.

Sam said a month later he received a letter from the family. The letter stated that they were about a hundred miles from home and tired of driving. Joe said, "I'll drive if you'd like." They all laughed and said it was nice for him to offer, but a blind driver would not relieve their fatigue. Joe said, "I've been afraid to say anything, but ever since I rolled down the neck of that horse in Tennessee, I've been able to see." I still get goose bumps when I think of that story.

Daughter Kim always promised she'd get me a Tennessee Walking Horse because riding one was like sitting in a rocking chair. I reckon at my present age, I'll just settle for the rocking chair.

* * * *

THE FEED STORE HORSE

In Jackson, a full-size model of a dapple-gray horse stood in the bay window of the feed store. It wore a saddle and bridle and looked like a champion to me. I often walked home from school through town, though it made the trip longer, just to admire the regal horse. I named him Smokey, as I did most animals that were colored gray.

The feed store evolved through a variety of enterprises until at last it became a florist shop. The florist removed the horse. There was public uproar: the horse lived in that window, it belonged in that window, put the horse back in the window, don't shop there until the horse is replaced in the window. Today the horse stands in the window, with calm countenance, amid beautiful bouquets that encircle and flatter its lovely ankles.

Its history is legendary. The text attached to the horse in the window:

Prince Truxton II, handmade of papier mache and wood frame, was purchased in 1889 from Horse Display Works of Dayton, Ohio. The dapple-gray horse stands 16 hands high and weighs some 600 pounds. (A hand equals four inches.) The mane and tail are of real horse's hair and the dark brown eyes are made of glass. The tail, chin and ears can be removed to fit a harness onto the horse.

Arriving on a railroad car here in Jackson, the horse cost $125 including the railway delivery charges. Its first home was in the building that housed the Albert Sander Hardware Co. on W. Main, where C. H. (Herman) Wolter had a harness shop. The horse was used to fit and display harnesses.

Situated on a platform with rollers, Wolter used to roll the display horse onto the sidewalk in front of the Harness Shop.

One day a herd of cattle was being driven through town on Main

Street to the railroad (not an uncommon sight in those days of the late 1800's). Suddenly a bull, maddened and upset, charged from the herd and rammed into the horse, pushing it down the sidewalk. Fortunately, the horse remained upright and was not damaged. From that day on, the horse was displayed in the window of the Harness Shop – a much safer location.

In 1898, C. H. Wolter completed a new building for his business. The horse was rolled down the hill to its new home and placed in the large front window.

It was not until Jackson's Sesquicentennial in 1965 that the horse officially received its name. Rebecca McDowell was the winner of the horse-naming contest during the celebration with the name of Prince Truxton II. After doing historical research, the name was suggested since Andrew Jackson, for whom the City of Jackson is named, owned a horse call Truxton which stood 15 hands 3 inches high. For many years prior to 1965, the horse in the window was simply referred to as Prince.

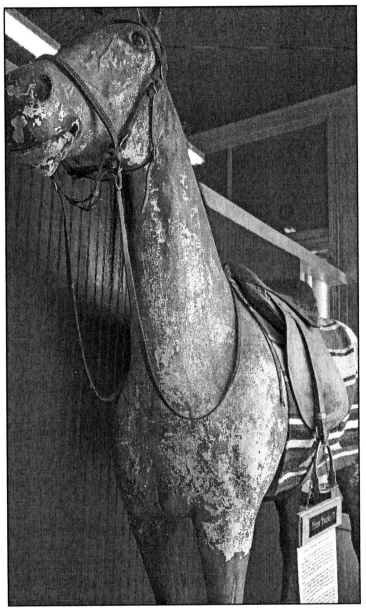

The feed store horse. Photo 2016.

*Jo and Judy on the front porch. That's the John Doggett
house in the background. Jackson, circa 1953.*

I am from playing Roy Rogers and Dale Evans during recess with Alta Faye

The King of the Cowboys and Queen of the West

A SHORT STORY ASSIGNMENT: write about something that happened at a young age. The story is based on true events.

Laying the long sticks side-by-side on the ground, I once more patiently explained to Alta Faye that the curved, slightly longer stick was, by default, Trigger. Therefore, the straighter non-distinguished stick was, by default, Buttermilk. She listened closely while observing my actions through skeptical doe-like eyes. We were two of the thirteen pupils that constituted the student body of the Limbaugh Public School, a one-room structure located several miles from Sedgesville, Missouri.

Alta Faye was my dearest friend, her only rival for my affections being the beautiful Idona, Alta Faye's older sister. We played Roy Rogers and Dale Evans, our favorite Saturday movie matinee heroes, during school recess and lunch breaks. Being a few inches taller, I was, by default, Roy, rider of the magnificent Trigger. Consequently, Alta Faye was, by default, Dale, and rode Buttermilk.

Occasional ridicule encouraged us to seek the privacy of the privy, often being rousted by a classmate in actual need of the facility. With great solemnity, we would saddle our sticks and ride off at high speed to right wrongs and foil potential corruption.

One autumn day, Walter Hartle, another second grader, beckoned us to follow him into the forbidden woods on the property perimeter. Walter was a friendly and trusted playmate.

We were ripe for adventure as we tethered our sticks to a tree. We followed Walter down the winding path that took us farther and farther from the sanctuary of the school yard. In the heavy shadows ahead we saw three of the eighth grade boys in a close cluster, busily engaged in an intense activity. Hearing our footsteps as we crunched decaying leaves on the forest floor, they turned and smiled at us in a most unpleasant manner. Slowly, they parted and stepped aside to reveal the progress of their endeavor.

The sight was horrifying! Hanging in a barren peach tree was a yellow and white striped cat. Utilizing vines, the cat was tied in a spread-eagle posture to the limbs. The curved branches beneath its backbone had stretched its abdomen taunt. It hissed and snarled in rage at its indigent dilemma as its strident harsh yowl demanded immediate release. The struggle with the cat had kicked up loose earth beneath the tree. The boys menacingly flicked supple limbs cut from a nearby Weeping Willow tree in the dust, creating a hazy cloud of fine particles that enveloped the scene.

The realization that they intended to flay the cat to death struck us like a physical blow. Sickened, I looked at Alta Faye; her eyes were silver-dollar round as she stared back at me. Her usually tan skin had dissipated to a pasty white color. Shock had rendered us mute. Simultaneously we mouthed the word: Run!

Our long fledgling legs flying, we hurled ourselves through the woods with reckless abandon so great was our fear and apprehension.

Breathless, we burst into the clearing and promptly spotted Idona sitting on the schoolhouse steps with my sisters, Jo and June. Babbling in soprano staccato voices that can only be interpreted by a sibling, we related the details of the imminent sacrifice of the feline victim. Our mutual sisters leaped to their feet and as one and tore into the school, instantly re-emerging with our teacher, Miss Mildred, in tow. We quickly lead our newly formed posse to the lynching site.

Hearing our rapid approach, the sneering boys spun to confront the interlopers causing interruption. With one sweeping glance,

Miss Mildred digested the scene and a look of dark thunder clouded her usually attractive visage. Fury! I had thought the cat was angry; Miss Mildred was incensed!

Observing her expression, Alta Faye and I, along with our combined sisters, fled the scene rather than invite associated guilt. After many anxious minutes, Miss Mildred and the chastised tormentors emerged from the forest, the boys shamefaced and their eyes cast downward. The boys mounted the steps and fanned out to stand in their assigned corners of the classroom as the rescued cat casually strolled out of the woods. Freed from its peril, he held his tail high, flicking it in eloquent circles. Daintily, he sat down in the shade and with delicate movements, began to bathe.

As we watched the cat wash, Alta Faye and I smiled at each other in satisfaction. Once again, by default, and by deed, Roy and Dale had confirmed that they were indeed - the King of the Cowboys and Queen of the West.

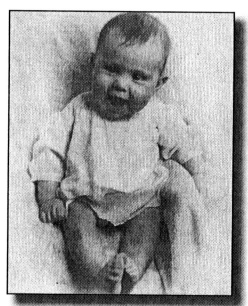

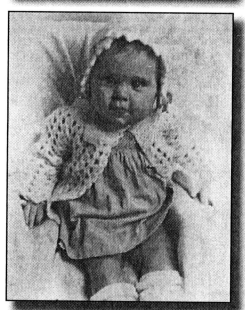

*Judy at six months. I still have this pink
and white sweater set.*

I am from living in Jackson, Missouri, city of beautiful homes, churches, schools and parks.

We moved into the Jackson house before it was totally completed. Daddy had arranged to borrow a cattle truck to transport the furniture from the farm to the new place. Unfortunately, the truck was used to haul cows the previous day and Daddy had to clean it up before he used it, so our beginning was delayed.

The move was scheduled over the Thanksgiving weekend. I was sick, so I was sent to Aunt Eula's to stay until after the afterwards. Jo had to go along to care for me, something she never let me forget because she missed out on everything.

Jackson Welcome Sign. Photo 2016.

June was sent with the first load of furniture. However, by the time the truck reached Jackson, she had forgotten where Mom said to put the different piece, so items were misplaced all over the house.

There was no front walk; just two long pieces of lumber to step on and to keep out of the mud. I cried one morning because I didn't want to go to school. Mom pointed out that I was in my underwear and the hired men were watching me through the windows. That night, there were sheets hung over the windows.

Mom and Daddy nailed quilts across the doorways to contain the sawdust while they sanded the floors in the living room and bedrooms. More labor at night after a full day on the job.

My parents and Grandma slept in the two downstairs bedrooms, and I slept on a day-bed in the living room. One night someone turned on the overhead light and strangers were walking through

Ruth Ann Talley and my sister on the front porch. Circa 1950, Jackson.
Note the wooden plank walkway.

the room. Then I saw my mother crying and I got scared. Somehow I knew something had happened to Grandma and I slipped to her room to check on her. She lay on her bed, very, very still. I went back to my bed to cry.

I later learned that Grandma had alerted Mom that something was wrong. We didn't have a telephone, so Daddy had gone to the next door neighbor to call an ambulance. He banged so hard on the door he broke the glass, but the ambulance arrived too late. It was a heart attack.

After Grandma passed, I was moved into her bedroom. There were three bedrooms on the second floor. Jo occupied the one facing Old Cape Road, and June was in the one overlooking the driveway. The third smallest bedroom housed the huge whole-house fan and lots of miscellaneous junk. It was referred to as the junk room. I took it over as a play room where I set up the electric train set, the building blocks, farm set and all the small horses I had collected. I played alone in that room for hours having a great time.

Eventually, I started sleeping in the junk room on one of the feather bed mattresses stored there. That ended when I awoke one morning to find a very large spider sleeping with, and on top of, me.

Before they were married, while living with Aunt Grace in Cape Girardeau, Mom had a chifferobe built for twenty dollars. It was a free-standing unit about four foot wide, seven feet high with a door with a catch. It had a clothes rod and high shelves for storage for all her clothes and shoes. It was moved into an upstairs bedroom in Jackson where it was filled with quilts, blankets, old curtains, etc.

Mom found Daddy emptying it one afternoon and asked what he was doing. He said, "Mom wants this." (My Grandma Linebarger.) Mom said she couldn't have it; she was using it for storage. Daddy pointed toward the area of the hallway wall and said he was going to build Mom closets out under the eaves. She told Daddy that when those closets were finished, Grandma could have the chifferobe. Daddy never got around to building the closets. However, Daddy did build Jo a cedar chest with her name spelled out on the front of it, and one for me that lasted for about twenty years.

The house in Jackson had a full concrete basement. It started beneath the front door and ended with the garage under the sun room. The only shower was located in a corner. In all the time we lived there, no curtains were put over the narrow windows. It was eerie at night to walk naked from the shower to the towel table. Maybe someone was looking in; maybe no one was. Finally Daddy built a couple of "modesty" walls for the shower. They were a plastic of some sort and about three inches wide, creating a very convenient shelf for shampoos and conditions.

93

As their grandchildren got older and began to visit the folks on their own, the hair care items were often forgotten. The number and variety of stuff was a smorgasbord to choose from. It was an opportunity to try a product that one didn't normally buy. It was common to see at least a dozen bottles setting on the shelf. Then came the visit when there was a single bottle. I needed to wash my hair and poured a small amount in the palm of my hand – it was a brown, gold, marbled thick substance. It was strange. It had a mixture of scents. It was rinsed from my hand without using it.

When I asked Mom about the bottle of shampoo in the shower, she said, "Oh, I got tired of all those bottle sittin' up there; I poured them all into just one."

Albert Sanders, of Sanders Hardware, lived three houses from us on Old Cape Road. His was a huge regal residence with a wide veranda porch that surrounded half of the structure. It had sliding pocket-doors, bay windows all over, a third-story attic, and a maid's stairway at the rear of the kitchen. The house had a stunning antique front door. My sister Jo bought the house with her husband, Dale. Many a stranger knocked at that front door and asked if they could buy it. She always said yes, but added that the house went with the door.

There was an exotic plant on one corner that had amazing plumes during the summer. Can you believe it; I now know the plant was pampas grass. Daddy eventually bought the old house to turn into apartments. He showed me the impressive staircase, which did not have a single knot hole. Before he could finish the renovation, a neighbor petitioned the city to make the street single-family residential zoning, which nixed his plans.

A full-sized barn and paddock for milk cows was located at the rear of the Sanders property. The barn was a warehouse for the hardware business and there was a loading dock filled with about twenty bottles of propane gas that the store also sold. Riding on those propane bottles made great pretend horses, plus we could change mounts mid-stream. About half an acre of land was nurtured as a vegetable garden. Their property was perfect for playing hide-and-

821 Old Cape Road, Jackson, MO.

seek, so many thrilling places to hide.

Albert's son, Bill Sanders, lived next door to him, two houses from us. Bill and May had twelve children, which explains the milk cows and garden. Some of their children were older than Jo and June and some were younger than I was. Boogie was the oldest and often wore blue jeans with holes in the rear sans underwear. I noticed that right away.

There was a set of twins, Lynn and Lane. Lynn had a problem and the back yard was fenced as soon as she was old enough to play outside. If someone started yelling "Lynnie's loose," everyone dropped what they were doing and went looking for her. One person would run to the creek, someone else toward the woods, and another in the direction of the highway. For a while her favorite thing was Mom's rocking chair. She would rock so hard the chair "walked" across the floor. I'd go tell the Sanders we had Lynnie and eventually walk her home.

Sanders had weeping willow trees and sometimes Lynn would make a whip out of a branch. I high-tailed it out of the yard and locked the fence gate because she knew how to nip you with it. And

95

don't ever let her see that you have a scab on your knee! She really enjoyed yanking those off.

We were situated within about ten miles of the Mississippi River at Cape Girardeau. We did a great deal of shopping there for the next larger town was St. Louis. The river flooded every spring and the stores on Main Street were ruined by the water.

The river freezes over every winter in the St. Louis area. All water traffic comes to a halt until the weather warms enough for the water to thaw.

In the olden days, the iced river was a no-man's land. Neither Missouri nor Illinois claimed judicial jurisdiction over the frozen river. In other words, there were no laws and no law enforcement.

Once the Mississippi was solid, a tent city blossomed in the middle of the river. Gambling houses, saloons, and brothels sprang up like mushrooms. Gaiety flourished nightly in a temporary sin city of "Anything Goes". When the creaking sounds of the ice changed tunes, it was an indication that it was time to head to shore – the ice was melting and would soon crack. Everyone packed up their profits and went home.

*I am from living in Jackson, Missouri, city of beautiful homes, **churches,** schools and parks.*

Friends and I were in and out of each other's church all the while we were growing up. I went to Vacation Bible School and if a friend's church did the same a week later, I'd go there too. I was welcomed in every place of worship and at nearly everyone ran into a friend's mother. If they were cleaning, we stayed and cleaned. If they needed tireless young legs to run hymnals all over the sanctuary, we did that.

We wandered into the buildings exploring areas that were

1809 Old Mckendree Chapel

seldom visited or just because we knew there was a drinking fountain. Ice cream socials were always in the church basements. Also wedding receptions, anniversary parties, baptism celebrations, anything you could get the church to approve was okay. During funerals, volunteers cooked and served a meal there for the bereaved family.

According to the website: In 1809 Old Mckendree Chapel was

established on two acres of land located in a grove of oak and maple trees. It is the oldest standing Protestant church structure west of the Mississippi River. With the cold spring running through the deep shade of the thick woods, it was an ideal location for camp meetings. In 1819 workmen built the chapel from poplar logs.

At some point, Daniel Boone worshiped there and carved his name into the back of one of the pews. Who knew he did graffiti?

Regular church services were held there until around 1890. Since then, the chapel has been reserved for special occasions. Eventually, an enormous shelter was constructed above it to protect it from the elements. After seeing a movie in Cape, it was a dark and starry place to go with your date to neck . . . or so I've heard. New Mcken-

Judy on Old Mckendree's steps. Circa 1958.

dree United Methodist Church is on High Street in Jackson, nearly opposite the Baptist Church. On Sunday mornings, the respective choirs would try to teach the church across the street how to sing the same hymn correctly.

Although already Methodists, after moving to town, Jo, June and I were required to attend meetings with the Methodist pastor, I never knew why. He gave us a pencil and a tablet to take notes and lectured us about the Bible.

June wrote "God" on her tablet and nodded at me to do the same. I wrote "god" and held it so she could see. With a fierce shake of her head, she again wrote "God." I wrote "god." I got another look of disgust. I didn't know what was wrong; I was spelling it the same way she did. The pastor grew frustrated observing our exchanges and released us. We didn't have to go see him anymore. Leave it to June.

I knew the Bible stories. While I ate breakfast with Daddy, he told me stories every day. He often acted them out and quizzed me afterwards. It was a great way to learn and having Daddy's undivided attention was so good it was fattening. One of my favorites was Samson. With his great hands, Daddy would grasp the pillars where the blinded Samson was chained and in a fury shoved them aside to destroy the temple and the wicked Philistines within.

As teenagers, my Baptist friends had many programs and prohibitions. A set number of Bible verses had to be memorized each week. Church attendance and participation in activities was necessary. Dancing and piercing any part of the body were not permitted.

The Catholic Church was on Highway 25. I attended a few times with a friend. I liked the small cushioned kneeling benches that flipped down from beneath the pew in front of ours. A woven round basket attached to a very long stick was passed to each member of the congregation from the aisle for the collection. It looked like a fireplace popcorn popper, but I put my nickel in anyway. A robed priest walked through the church swinging a lantern that perfumed the air.

The red brick Lutheran Church was near the schools. I also visited there, and quickly learned not to get too comfortable because we stood and sat, stood and sat throughout the entire service.

On summer nights we'd drive out on a country gravel road to a bridge that had a long approach in both directions. Cars would be parked at either end of the bridge facing each other.

Headlights lit the smooth bridge surface and car radios tuned to the same station on high volume provided the music. Bridge dancing was lots of fun and many of my partners at these spontaneous

Judy with Skipper Kelley. Jackson side porch. Circa 1958.

events were of the Baptist persuasion.

A Teen Town opened on the second floor of a bar and pool hall called Blick's. It was furnished with a Ping-Pong table, books, chess and checker sets, snacks, and of course music and a chaperone. We knew Baptist kids loved to dance – we'd see them on the bridge, but many of them weren't allowed to go to Teen Town.

When I turned sixteen, I wanted to drive the family car, a two-toned Pontiac. A guaranteed way to get it was to go to Sunday School and church. On Sunday, I would pick up Patty Niblack and after services we cruised all the hang-outs to see who was out and about. Mom complained that if she sent me for a loaf of bread, ten miles were added to the odometer by the time I came home. Jo and June were not allowed to drive the family car while they still lived at home; I took it to school my senior year. It helps when your older siblings wear down your folks.

*Judy with nephew Ricky Schneier (Jo's), left, and nephew
Skipper Kelley (June's), right. Circa 1958, Jackson.*

Our church, the New Mckendree Methodist, had lovely stained-glass windows depicting biblical scenes like the Last Supper, Christ praying in the Garden of Gethsemane, and Christ being deposed from the cross. There was a very impressive organ, always played by Mrs. Ellis, who was also my grade school music teacher. This poor lady tried in vain to acquaint us with the classics, but unless it was *William Tell Overture* (the Lone Ranger's theme music), we yawned through it.

Communion was always an interesting and moving experience. We were directed in small groups to the front of the church and knelt on a padded cushion at the railing. As someone walked by, you would open your mouth and a wafer was placed on your tongue.

At many churches a common chalice was used to serve each person a sip of wine or grape juice. The rim was wiped with a cloth and then presented to the next person.

June, Me and Jo. Jackson driveway, circa 1953.

The Episcopal Church served real wine and fresh-baked warm bread. Eventually, tiny plastic glasses replaced the chalice.

While an Episcopalian, I volunteered one Saturday a month to work in the church sacristy. We replaced the altar candles, vacuumed the area behind the rail, polished brass fixtures and prepared the vestments the priest would wear the next morning.

A table was in place to receive his raiment. First the long satin sash he wore around his neck was folded into an "H" shape on the table. Next, the white rope that would encircle his waist was doubled and formed into an "S." A hassock was put down and folded so that when the hem was lifted the garment could slide right over his head. An under tunic was added and then everything was covered with a white cloth in case the ceiling shed any particles that would soil his garments. These items were worn over his white shirt, tie and slacks.

My priest at that time eventually left the Episcopal Church and went to the Catholic Church in the Carolinas. It was unprecedented for a married Episcopal priest with five children to become a Catholic priest, but it happened.

From left, Wanda Morrison, Me, Ruth Ann Talley with June in back. Note the cowboy boots. That's Harry Talley's cattle truck behind us, which is parked about the same place where Smokey and I climbed beneath it the day we met. Circa 1953.

I changed denominations, too. I still remember the feel of water trickling down my back when I was baptized in the Methodist Church in Sedgesville. I was baptized again in the Methodist Church in Jackson, a Baptist Church in Mentor, Ohio, and an Episcopal Church in Akron, Ohio. I may do something so terrible I'm denied entrance to Heaven, but it won't be because I wasn't sprinkled enough.

Judy - high school graduatioon picture, age 16.

I am from living in Jackson, Missouri, city of beautiful homes, churches, **schools** and parks

The Jackson Elementary School was a brick, two-story structure. A gymnasium would eventually be built across the street. The high school was on the adjacent block with the Home Economics/Future Farmers/Music building across the street from it. A cemetery was in the next block. When we stayed late for club meetings or other after school activities, we ran past the cemetery on the way home, just in case.

When we moved to town and started school, Mom worried that Jo or June might have a problem adjusting to their new environment, with little concern about me. That proved to be a gross miscalculation.

The first day of school, Mom walked me to my second grade classroom while Jo and June climbed the stairs to the second floor. When Mom started to leave, I began crying, so she spent the day.

The following morning, as we crossed the school's threshold, I firmly planted my feet and refused to take another step. That hard-hearted woman grabbed my hand and started dragging me down the corridor while I cried and begged to go home. Mom took a determined hold on both my hands. The harder she pulled, the louder I screamed. It was one of those magical moments one never forgets.

My second grade teacher had never experienced a student quite like me. Poor Mrs. Wagner partially filled a rusty three-pound Maxwell House coffee can with water and got a nasty rag. She dipped the rag in the water, wrung it out, then washed and washed my face while I sobbed. All the while, my stewing mother sat on a grade-school-sized chair in the back of the classroom staring at the clock and worrying her purse strap with her fingers. At 10:00 on the dot, she slipped out of the classroom. But, she'd been observed, and I started howling afresh. Without conscience, she abandoned me

Jo, who taught me to read

to the terror. I'd never been left on my own before. Mrs. Wagner asked a girl named Frances to escort me to the bathroom. When I flushed the toilet, Frances asked me how I knew to do that since I was from the country. I told her my aunt had one. Another girl, Sandra, leaned over as she passed my desk and whispered "Bawl Baby!" Frances and I were friends all through school. I still dislike Susan.

There were about hirty children in that class and I didn't know any of them. Earlier Mom had pointed at a kid named Billy Huckstep and said he was a distant cousin, which did nothing to calm me. Meanwhile, Jo and June sat on the second floor musing with everyone else as to the identity of that screaming child. They disavowed all knowledge of me.

I have no idea how my behavior was explained to my classmates. Maybe Mrs. Wagner told them I was a wild child since my flushing a toilet provoked comment. However, no one, other than Snotty Susan, was ever unkind to me.

This went on for weeks and weeks. I had never been put through something like that before. In retrospect, I'm surprised I wasn't punished or spanked for my behavior. I guess Mom knew that my fear was genuine.

Mrs. Wagner was not feeling blessed either. In addition to the face washings, she had to print my last name, Linebarger, on the blackboard because I didn't know how to spell it. For the first time, it was necessary to put my name on every blasted thing I did. At the country school, I didn't have papers; I just recited my lessons to Miss Mildred.

One day Mrs. Wagner asked if anyone knew the Roman numerals? I did. Stupidly, I raised my hand and she called me to the front of the class. I got to three correctly. When I said four – IIII, Richard

Conley who was sitting directly in front of me, began to shake his head. I started crying and went to my desk.

Later that year Richard stabbed me in the wrist with a pencil. I can still see a speck of the dark lead embedded there. I don't recall why that happened as Richard is a very sweet boy and now, man. Perhaps he was not a fan of crying girls. I was so shy that I had attended school for two months before I ever went out the back door to the playground for fear of getting lost. It was like, hey, swings, monkey bars, balls! Who knew they had great stuff out there?

At the end of each day, I waited at the bottom of the stairs for Jo and June and we walked the mile home together. One day they were late and I had no idea how to get home, so, you guessed it, the torrent of tears began. When they at last appeared they gave me an earful for crying, but they were never late again. Sisters are easily embarrassed at ages twelve and thirteen. The only relief from the trauma of
school came when we returned home. Along with Daddy, the carpenters were still building the house. It was livable but required lots of finishing on both the exterior and interior. We girls had the job of gathering all the bent nails the workers threw to the ground and hammer them straight again. They went back into the supply bin and were re-issued the next day. Life was great for me, until the school door opened in the morning.

And then, one day, God spoke to me.

I was using the pencil sharpener near Mrs. Wagner's desk when a deep baritone voice asked, "May I have your attention, please?" I immediately went to my desk and sat down to listen. I was astonished by my classmates' demeanor. Some were whispering, some using scissors, and some, for Pete's sake, were coloring! Such disrespect jolted me.

God proceeded to tell me to let my folks know that there would be a PTA meeting on Wednesday night, to be sure I put my name on my lunch ticket, and to pick up any litter on the playground and put it in the trash barrel.

That's the day I quit crying.

Not until years later did I learn what a public address system is.

HIGH SCHOOL
DIVERSIFIED OCCUPATION

The Jackson High School system required so many credits to graduate – thirty-six, I think. A biology class, my favorite, was worth one credit, four years of English classes were worth four credits, etc.

Students had to be at least in their junior year to participate in the Diversified Occupation program. A merchant in Jackson, such as a jewelry shop or clothing store, would hire the student to work in their business for a semester. I worked at Jackson Dry Cleaners for Paul Beattie.

On the day the photo below was taken, Mom had casually mentioned, "I bet Uncle Fred shows up today, and I bet he has a brand new car." A few hours later, Uncle Fred showed up in said brand new car. I concluded Mom was clairvoyant. Circa Jackson, 1955.

I left school each day at 1:00 PM and worked at the cleaners until 5:00 PM. I was paid less than $1 per hour, but gained experience working with the public. I was responsible for closing out the cash register, hiding the money bag beneath a loose board, and closing the shop.

Paul taught me to do invisible weaving on men's sports jackets and slacks. If a button was loose on a blouse or shirt, I removed it and sewed it back on snug. I went through the pockets of all garments left for processing and often found wallets and change, in addition to lipsticks, folded notes, handerchiefs (which were dry-cleaned) and kleenex (which were thrown out). Everything was placed in a bag labeled with the customer's name and hung on the hanger with the clothing.

Numerous pieces for the same client were wired together with a little twist tie so nothing would be misplaced. If there was an item elsewhere, such as a boxed hat on a shelf, it was noted on the ticket.

A married couple also worked there, pressing clothes on a large steam mangle. It was a hinged clam-shell like device that was padded top and bottom. A pair of trousers was placed on the padded surface, the top portion was closed down by hand using a handle and steam was forced through the fabric by means of a foot pedal.

After a wedding, usually the bride's mother would bring in the worn-once white wedding dress for cleaning. Paul would remove it from the hanger, hold it up straight, lift it as though the bride was still within, and then wad the entire dress into the huge vat containing cleaning solution. After pressing, it was wrapped in tissue paper and folded into a large rectangular cedar-lined box and sealed. If the bride had seen it go swimming in the brown liquid of the vat she would have probably had heart failure.

The first winter I worked there, I read *War and Peace* by Tolstoy. I placed the book and my hands on the lower mangle pad where residual heat warmed them. I also read *The Virginian* by Owen Wister; however, no one could quite read the title correctly and I kept having to explain that it wasn't *The Virgin*. I think they were messing with a young girl.

Dropped off orders were given a pick-up date three days hence. In reality, the process was much quicker. My boyfriend gave me his coat one day at lunch and I returned it to him that evening, cleaned. All the dry cleaning for my family was done for free.

Mrs. Loman, the mother of a classmate and one-time Sunday

*Uncle Limey, Grandma Linebarger and Daddy in
Cape Girardeau, circa 1956.*

School teacher, had a shoe store that I walked by on the way home. I developed a passion for her darling shoes and rarely made to the house with an entire paycheck.

Mr. Nelson taught Diversified Occupation. In addition to work-place protocal, we learned to do income taxes, establish a budget for assets and expenditures, and obtained a social security card.

Mr. Nelson, a man of many talents, also taught driver's training. Brennecks Chevrolet in Jackson donated a new car each year to be used for that class. Much to Mr. Nelson's dismay, it was not equipped with a second steering wheel and brake pedal. We were grateful it had power steering and an automatic transmission, otherwise we would have bucked all over town.

I had spent hours in our car pretend driving and was familiar with the dashboard and driving principles. Most of the other students were not. Consequently, we drove into many, many yards and over curbs.

Also a licensed pilot, Mr. Nelson sometimes flew emergency mercy flights from Cape Girardeau to St. Louis hosiptals. He was paid with flying hours by the airport. One afternoon he used some of those hours to invite three of us to fly with him. No permission slips, no liability waivers. It was wonderful. We flew low over each of our homes, and he even let me take the wheel. I was thrilled. However, my friend Saundra Smith was in the back seat retching and trying not to lose her lunch.

After an overnight stay in the country when we brushed our teeth by the cistern and spit the foam onto the ground, poor Saundra would be turning green and retchingat the sight of it. The plane ride had much the same effect.

I was dating a boy who was studying to be a chemical engineer at the University of Missouri in Columbia.So I enrolled in a chemistry class. I envisioned that we would sit before a fire in the evening discussing formulas. I had taken an algerbra class, but no higher math courses. During the algerbra class, I had often placed my extra text books on the open window sill (no air-conditioning) and when opportunity arrived, I would knock them out the window. I would ask permission to go fetch them, and en route snack on a banana or apple. Algerba was so easy it worked for awhile. By the time I realized it was actually hard, it was a struggle to catch up.

The first day of chemistry, I thought they must have given me the wrong textbook because the discussion by the teacher did not coincide with what I was reading. Mass, volume, pressure and more Greek-to-me-stuff.

The girl beside me, Carol Long, started a game by asking me what time it was. My desk didn't face the clock. I got to be uncanny at counting time in my head and was usually within a minute. Carol was especially fun because her sister had a convertible that Carol often borrowed on Sunday afternoons. There was always three or four of us eager to join her for a joy ride..

I stayed after class for tutoring and my boyfriend helped me. When I occasionally got a problem correct, I had to explain my processing to the teacher. He conceded that I had the correct answer but disputed the method employed to reach it.

I was failing miserably when an assignment was given to write a seven-page typed paper on a subject dealing with chemistry. The paper would count for one-half our grade in the class. My approved subject was Narcotics.

There were rumors that marijuana had been found in Sikeston, a city forty miles from us. It might as well have been the moon. We didn't know what that was or what it was for, we were busy trying to scrape up twenty-five cents to buy cigarettes from the laundry mat vending machine.

Encyclopedias, magazines, periodicals, I researched everything I could get my hands on. I started out carefully restating each sentence, but eventually abandoned all original writing and copied text straight out of the books. I ended up with seventy type-written pages and got an A+. The teacher carried my paper around for a week showing it to anyone who would look at it. I passed the class for that semester and cancelled the following one.

When we cleaned out the Jackson house upstairs junk room, we found that Mom saved that paper for me.

Somehow, no one noticed that I didn't schedule a replacement class for that hour. My teacher friend, Mr. Nelson would stand outside the principal's office, which had a glass wall, and note when Mr. Lamont, the principal, went to his private area. Mr. Nelson

Miss Judy Linebarger, daughter of Mr. and Mrs. Everett Linebarger entertained Saturday night with a Halloween bunking party. The party continued on until morning when the girls went to church. During the evening the girls went "trick or treating" and played games after returning home. The guests were, Misses Sharon Sievers, Donna Byrd, Nancy Deweese, Saundra Smith, Kay Randol, Betty Sievers, Sharon Armstrong, Vicki Aufdenberg, Barbara Palisch, Jane Schade, Mary Schoen, Carolyn Hutteger, Sandy LaPierre, Rita White and Judy Lincoln.

Cash-Book newspaper article about one of the bunking parties. Circa 1960.

Mom with Uncle Ode's car, circa 1930.

would signal me that the coast was clear and I would brazenly stroll by, go to my car and drive home to see if I had received a letter from my boyfriend. I returned to school in time for the next class.

The best entertainment put on by the high school was the Junior play, which was usually a comedy. I was in *The Egg and I* by Betty MacDonald. It's about a city girl that marries a country boy and moves to his chicken ranch. I played the younger child, a smart-mouthed daughter, a departure from my real life.

Mom and Jo attended the play (Daddy didn't fit comfortably in the auditorum seats) which by design ran for one performance. Mom sewed four different wardrobe changes for me. Her work may have inspired the judges because I won the Dramatic Award that year.

Mr. Nelson came to our high school reunion party around year twenty. He gave me his business card which read: Retired Full-time Philospher.

Judy – Second grade.

I am from living in Jackson, Missouri, city of beautiful homes, churches, schools and parks

Receiving a hand-me-down bicycle opened new worlds for me. Until then, I walked everywhere I wanted to go. No longer did I have to wait until Mom had time to run me to Gaitha Godwin's house to read comic books (that dear woman would just sit in the car for an hour while I devoured comics), or to the library to borrow a book.

Now independent, I'd watch Miss Bess, the librarian, pull the title card from the little pocket on the book's inside page. Then she'd dip her great pen in the jar of black India ink and carefully write "215" on my card, my check-out number. I felt very grown up peddling home while grasping a book around the handlebar.

The City Park was located three miles from our house. There were basketball and tennis courts, swings, numerous picnic areas, seesaws, paths, dirt and paved roads, and a huge swimming pool. Surrounded by a ten-foot high chain-link fence, the local police patrolled the pool nightly.

While a teenager, there were rumors of kids climbing the fence at night after the pool closed.

Daddy warned, "I better never catch you climbing that fence!"

I said, "Don't worry, Daddy, you'll never catch me."

It was several years before he finally registered what I had said. I was in that pool nearly every night. When the police cruiser drove through, we all hid in the shadows cast on the deep end by the diving boards.

Hubble Creek meandered along the edge of the park creating a shallow waterway with an abundance of moss-covered rocks. The property on the opposite bank belonged to a drive-in movie theater. While dusk deepened, before the movie could be shown, the drive-in offered pony rides to children. The Shetland ponies were stabled in an enclosure by the creek.

About once a week, my friend Ruth Ann and I selected one of the belts belonging to our dads and biked to the park. After wadding the creek, we'd climb the barbed-wire fenced corral and catch a pony. The belt became a one-reined halter over the irritated pony's nose.

Shetland ponies hate children, all children, but especially, us children. They couldn't get rid of us. They would run as close to the barbed-wire as possible to scrape us from their backs. They are nasty mean little buggers but the closest thing we had to a horse. We became very adroit at riding with one leg raised up into the air on the dangerous barbed-wire side of the little fiends.

When the hosiery mill whistle blew loud and clear at 4:00, we'd release the ponies in peace and head for home.

At the time, the bike provided other escapes from our house on Old Cape Road, the only paved road to Cape Girardeau. A near-by residence on the street had been the toll-house. One room projected outward where a window could be opened to accept the five cent tolls from drivers. When the construction of the road was paid off, Mr. Brotherton, the toll taker, bought the property as his home.

I would often visit the Johnson place located across the street from the toll-house. They possessed a player piano. I was not invited; I just knocked on the door and asked if I could play the piano. In summer, all the doors and windows were open to the silence of the street. I would pedal furiously while the inserted roll spun out "Beautiful Dreamer." It would get very quiet again, and then I'd hear Mr. Brotherton shout, "Play it again, Judy." I've wondered about Nestle Toll House Cookies - whether the name had to do with a similar situation.

Ruth Ann Talley lived directly across the street. Her daddy was a city farmer. They lived in town but had fields for various purposes in the country with lots of grazing stock. We occasionally rode one of his dairy cows, which hurt because of its uncomfortable backbone. We were scolded because running the cow made the milk clot. Who wants to ride a walking cow?

Mom got off work at the shoe factory in Cape at 4:00 and would be home by 4:30. Mom had a lead foot and could actually be home much earlier. I needed to put Daddy's belt back before she caught me with it. That woman had a sixth
sense about what I'd been up to and the tiniest clue would give me away.

Although, she never mentioned that I smelled like horse.

Hubble Creek in Jackson City Park. The drive-in ponies were stabled on the left bank side. Photo 2016.

WASHING DISHES

It might seem unusual in a farm setting, that a kitchen table covered with an old worn oilcloth was set with cups and saucers for breakfast. In our case, it was just part of the breakfast routine; mugs had not become popular yet except in diners and truck stops.

I began drinking coffee as a toddler. It was poured into a cup with generous quantities of sugar and cream. My coffee was saucered for me so it would cool enough for me to sip from it. (A small portion was poured from the cup into its saucer.) I slurped it from the saucer until I was capable of lifting the saucer and drinking from it. After a great deal of blowing across the surface, I graduated to drinking from the cup like everyone else, although occasionally adults drank hot liquid from a saucer as well.

Before I was old enough to pour boiling water into a basin, I was assigned a turn to wash dishes. On the farm dishes were washed in a large metal dented much-used pan, dried and put away. After moving to town, they were washed in the kitchen sink, air-dried in the adjacent sink, and put away before starting the next meal.

In the summer, Jo babysat two little boys in the country while June babysat two kids in town who were older than me. With Mom and Daddy also at work, I was left on my own all day, a circumstance I really enjoyed. There was usually a pot of rice left on the stove for breakfast, or cereal to start the day. I played with Butch and Lonnie Wilcox who lived across the street. I was slightly older, and therefore, the leader of our miniature gang.

I loved to play at their house because one of them had a pair of cowboy boots that I lusted after and wore every chance I got. They were too small and nearly crippled me but they were Cowboy Boots! Once I kicked a football with them on and jammed my big toe. Daddy had me look up at the ceiling while he gave my toe a yank to set it right. It hurt like the dickens but jerked the joint back into place.

Wilcox's yard had a grape arbor and we'd feast on the ripe fruit. They rented the house from the Talley family who lived next door and had a large garden that included a strawberry patch. Folks just

June, Jo and Judy, on the farm. Circa 1947.

down the road had both an apple and a peach orchard. We were seldom hungry, and let's face it, stolen fruit *is* delicious. Butch and Lonnie also had a baby brother, Kurt, and a Great Dane named King that I adored and exercised.

When the Hosiery Mill blew its 4:00 whistle, Butch, Lonnie and I headed for my house. I quickly started the dish water for one of the boys, gave the other a mop for the kitchen floor, and ran around making beds. When the chores were finished, I cut a slice of cake (Mom perpetually made cakes) for each of us and we went back outside to play.

Once, my mother, who had rags for everything, bought a sponge. Cleaning with it was delightful. When the boys weren't with me, I'd use the sponge to wipe the coffee circles out of the saucers and put them in the cabinet. The rest of the dishes had to go into soapy water to remove dried egg yolks and gravy from them.

Daddy smoked at the table and had a tendency to put his cigarettes out in his plate. Nasty unfiltered Camel cigarettes – horrible things to learn to smoke on - made one spit tobacco bits

119

everywhere, or so I've heard.

Eventually, Mom noticed the saucers had sort of a film on them and questioned me about it. I suggested that the cabinet was very, very hot and the saucers were sweating in there. Thereafter, everything went into the soapy water.

After supper, I'd be washing dishes while Mom cleared the table. I'd feel her hand slip beneath my arm and slid the dish that had held mashed potatoes into the water. That meant she'd put the leftover potatoes into a smaller bowl. Soon the dish that had held tomatoes slid in. Then the meat platter. The cornbread pan. The tea pitcher. The butter knife. The jelly jar lid. All the leftovers were put into smaller containers to be served again the next night. Plus, all the tiny bowls that had been taken from the fridge that night had to be washed. By the time I got to the pots and skillets, I had a mountain of dishes draining and struggled to find a toehold for the remaining items.

When my son Jefferson was about eight, he stood in the Jackson kitchen door and announced to my mother, "Grandma, I don't eat leftovers." Mom said, "That's good to know, Jeff."

Innocent child didn't know he was having leftovers every night combined into a new dish, as well as turkey wieners and two percent milk. I would fill the sink with dishes for Jeff to clean and give him a turkey baster to use. He'd wash dishes forever; I just had to mop the floor afterwards.

I hated canning season because the empty containers had to be re-washed. My hand was the smallest, so guess who had to do the pint jars? All the paraphernalia that accompanied preserving food had to be washed before and after use. There was a large metal cone-shaped device with holes up and down its cylinder that set over a pan with the small part at the bottom. Mom poured cooked tomatoes into it and used a wooden pestle to squeeze all the juice through the holes and into the pan. The juice was jarred and went into a pressure cooker that held eight quarts maximum. Tomatoes for side dishes were first blanched, the peels removed, and then canned whole.

Green beans were brought into the house from the garden in a bushel basket. Everyone got a tray full and went to the sun room where the TV was located. With the trays on our laps, we'd string beans and cut out bug bites, then snap them, all the while watching "Gunsmoke" or "Bonanza." We also had lots and lots of hully beans.

Cucumbers were fashioned into canned pickles and added to the storage in the basement. The shelves were three or four feet deep and ran down one wall. The canning date was written on the top of each lid with the oldest dates being eaten first, no matter how much you whined that it was outdated. The shelves contained three to five years of processed fruits and vegetables.

A plum tree grew just beyond the back boundary of our yard. The

Grandma Looney with her brothers,
Robert (left) and Fred (right) Hartle

owner didn't nurture or want the fruit, so Mom gathered the plums yearly. The tree produced such an abundance that she propped the lower limbs up with spare wooden 2 x 4's to keep the boughs from breaking. We'd have plum preserves all winter.

We didn't have air-conditioning then, just a monster fan in the junk room window upstairs. One had to reach through the fan blades to open the window behind it and walk across the room to plug it in. It moved a tremendous volume of air but the windows were only opened a few inches to keep a breeze moving all over the house. During the canning season and holiday meals, the kitchen was a burning hell hole. Even a huge fan couldn't thwart that.

When Jo moved her family a few doors away on Old Cape Road,

Mom, Grandma Looney, and Mom's sister, Aunt Grace.

her five children were at the house all the time. The fan was a source of concern for small curious fingers, so Daddy resurrected Tall Katy.

Tall Katy was invented during a visit to Jesse and Rainey Hartle's house in the country. The Hartle house was a brick two-story and we were very curious about the second floor. Mom had to check on us to make sure we didn't go exploring. So Daddy made up Tall Katy, who was very tall and rail thin. She had a wicked long nose with warts and dressed in black head to toe. Her hair was covered with a black scarf and she moved without sound. Most importantly, she hated little children. We would stand at the bottom of Jesse and Rainey's stairs craning our neck to catch a glimpse of her, but never did. Neither did we ever place a foot beyond the first step.

When any of the kids looked up the stairway toward the fan, Daddy would tell them that Tall Katy was up there and didn't want to be disturbed. He went on with scary tales of how mean Tall Katy could be when riled. (This was the same Jesse and Rainey whose house and farm were destroyed by the tornado.)

Washing dishes was altogether a different chore for holiday occasions when the house filled with family. All the women helped in the kitchen, both with the cooking and the cleaning up. Children played outside while the adults ate. Then the table was cleared and re-set with the leftovers for the kids. If the adults stayed at the table too long laughing and telling jokes, eventually, the children made themselves a plate and found a place to eat. In time, a kids table was set up, a dandy arrangement that still exists.

I always enjoyed washing dishes at someone else's house. I liked seeing different plates and silverware, their glasses and cups. It was much more interesting and now that I think of it, an excellent opportunity to snoop into other people's kitchen. Good grief, I'm nosey!

When I was about ten, I went up the street to Deal's Nursing Home and asked for a job washing dishes. They were not hiring children at that time, so I walked back home unemployed. Mom always told that story with amusement, like I wasn't serious, but I was looking for wages. She had a fit when I told her I'd gone to the

Mary Edith Hartle Looney, Grandma.

Keenland racehorse stable at the end of Old Cape Road and asked to wash the horses. She twisted her apron and asked with aston-ishment, "With all those men?" I said, "No, with all those horses." Apparently, the horse farm and nursing shared the same underage employment policy.

The summer I stayed with my grandparents, Aunt Oma would come regularly and criticize the condition of the washed dishes in the cabinets, the way I ironed the pillowcases, and the fact that I hadn't swept the back porch. Dang! She would pull a glass from the back of the shelf and using a long accusing finger, she's wipe a mark through the film on the surface. I hadn't used that one, so I hadn't washed that one. Give me a break lady!

One summer when Jo stayed with our grandparents, Grandpa

wouldn't allow her to use dish detergent in the wash water. She'd wash and dry the dishes and put them away. Grandpa would walk up Pearl Street to visit Uncle Howard. Then Grandma would have Jo take out all the dishes she'd just put away and wash them again with soap. Old people!

The only thing worse than washing canning supplies was cleaning up after sausage making. That meat grinder just refused to come clean. Greasy pork doesn't surrender easily.

I even washed dishes after Eastern Star meetings.

Mom with Uncle Fred Hartle, Grandma Looney's
brother. On the farm, Circa 1925.

MOM'S DISHES

My husband Gene and I went to Missouri about every six months. The trip had a dual purpose, to do repair/maintenance, cleaning, and whatever at the house, and to give Jo a break from looking after Mom.

Domed glass dish.

During one such trip, I was doing dishes and Mom said, "You know, used to, each summer I would wash every dish in the cabinets."

I asked, "Would you like me to wash the dishes for you?"

"Oh, no," she said. "You're on vacation."

We had been on the roof clearing debris, repairing gutters, replacing wood rot boards and raking leaves. I had yet to do anything I would call a 'vacation' activity.

Next day, Mom mentioned the dishes again and once more a few days later. Each time I offered to wash them all and she protested it was too much work.

When Daddy built the kitchen cabinets, he included three sets of what-not shelves. They were little half-moon sets of shelves on

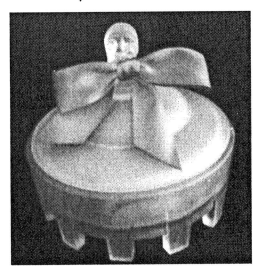

Safety pin bowl.

either side of the kitchen window and at the end of the cabinets at the stove. The shelves were intended to hold things like the cooking salt and pepper shakers, hot pads, juice glasses, etc. Small items that need not live inside the cabinets.

I could see her assortment had "stuff" collected on them because of their proximity to the heat and grease in the kitchen. I asked if it would be okay if I just washed the items on the what-not shelves. Well, that sounded dandy to her.

After the what-nots, I suggested I do the first shelf in each cabinet that housed the dishes she handled most often – meat platter, cereal bowls, coffee cups, etc. That was dandy as well. Without discussion, from there I worked my way up the shelves around the entire kitchen.

There was another row of cabinets at the tip-top of the kitchen, right at the ceiling. I got a stool, climbed onto the cabinet top and opened the first door.

Glass lidded candy dish.

It was El Dorado. It was Sutter's Mill, the Hope Diamond, Ali Baba's secret "open sesame" cache of treasure. Dishes stacked within that I only had a vague memory of ever seeing before. I carefully loaded them onto the countertop and began washing again.

Who knows the original owner of the items? My great grandmother died young leaving my grandmother to raise her five siblings. Grandma would have used the same pieces. And my mother lived in the same farm house as well. Possession passed with the generations and farmhouse occupancy.

Wonderful heavy glass bowls on pedestals that had companion glass domes that set on top. Saucers and platters that were so thin I could have read the newspaper through them. Cut-glass vases and decanters. Ornate molds for just-churned butter. An actual saltcellar.

Looking at them glittering in the sunlight through the kitchen window, Mom uttered the fateful phrase: "If you want any of these dishes, take them." ("Ode to Joy" plays in background.) I had never been at the head of a line that Jo and June had not already traversed! Hot damn! I was first up with the dishes.

Fruit Dish

In the upstairs junk bedroom was a piece of old furniture. On one side was a door that opened so clothes could be hung inside. The other side had a shelf with a mirror above it and three drawers below it. A large box of photographs was stored inside. One day Mom had suggested I go through them and take any photos that I wanted – Jo and June had already gone through them. I sorted through the remaining pictures, most blurred and out-of-focus with half of a person cut off, and found an assortment that I have used in this book.

Another time Mom suggested. I go through the phonograph re-

Glass Serving Platter

cords in the living room and take what I wanted – Jo and June had already been through them. I searched and took artists I'd actually heard of and a large number of classical records that had been a gift with the purchase of the record player. They had never been played.

This trip, I had taken home artificial flowers to make arrangements for Mom, hers were looking pretty dim. She had a green

Pedestal dish.

thumb for real plants and on a large revolving table in the living room where about twenty African Violets were growing. Her only task to produce more of them was to lay a leaf on a new pot of soil and they would begin to develop. She had a Peace Lily in the sun room that sat on a bookcase in front of a window. When she could see through the plant to the outside, she knew it needed water.

I'd transported the artificial flowers in two large sturdy paper ream boxes stuffed with newspaper that were ideal for packing dishes. I set all the dishes I wanted on the living room carpet and had Mom look them over. She surveyed the twinkling glass and said, "Take them all." I wrapped each piece carefully in newspaper and repacked the boxes with treasure for the ride back to Florida.

Having stowed my loot, I got back on the countertop and repacked the upper-most cabinet. I left many beautiful wished-for pieces, because logically, eventually I would also get one-third of

Lidded pedestal dish.

what I left behind. Then I moved random pieces from lower shelves to make it crowded as it was initially.

In Florida I put the pieces away, displaying many of them like works of art around the house.

After Mom passed away, I took a spice cabinet hanging on the kitchen wall that Daddy had made Mom. It was the only furnishing that would fit in the car. It had an enormous bolt holding it on the wall. I asked Jo if she knew why Daddy used such a large bolt - it was because that was the one he had.

Mom loved her flowers. Jackson.

I am from listening to summer night concerts when my dad sang and played his guitar on the side porch steps.

I don't know how old Daddy was when he acquired the second-hand Gibson guitar in the picture. It has a two-digit manufacture's number stamped on the interior body, 34 I think. It came with a black cardboard carrying case, the bottom filled with sheet music.

To go with his second-hand guitar, he crafted his own picks

Daddy on the side steps of the house in Jackson, Circa 1960.

from plastic. He was elated when unsolicited credit cardsarrived – he could cut new picks from the colorful plastic. Daddy courted Mom with the Gibson and entertained their friends on Sundays at the Cape Rock.

By the time he was in his early seventies, Daddy's hearing was poor. Mom had finally convinced him to buy a set of false teeth (he was thrilled to bite through lettuce again) but he wouldn't agree to wearing hearing aids.

During a trip to Missouri, he admired my portable cassette player, noting that it had earphones. I put in a Patsy Cline tape (who doesn't love Patsy?) and showed him how to adjust the volume to hear every word. Needless to say, the tape player remained in Missouri with Daddy. The very idea that he could play it loudly without disturbing Mom was fantastic for him, and her.

Daddy had amassed quite a media operation that he moved to the basement in an attempt to save Mom's sanity. She liked music, but not at the volume he required. Daddy read an ad in the newspaper placed by a man who had been involved in the radio business. He

Daddy and a fellow musician at Cape Rock. Circa 1935.

was selling blank eight-track and cassette tapes at a bargain price. Daddy drove to Cape, met the man and bought out his inventory. Half way back home, he realized he was having a heart attack.

There are only seven miles between Jackson and Cape so he elected to keep on going. In the meantime, Mom had gotten worried because he was gone so long. She kept looking for him through the Venetian blinds on the window in the sunroom that overlooked the driveway. Little did she know he had driven down the driveway and around the house through the back yard to the side door steps.

The neighbors saw the car in the yard and noticed Daddy sitting on the steps hugging his chest. They alerted Mom, who flew out of the house, put Daddy into the car passenger seat and drove him to St. Francis Hospital in Cape. It was a twenty-minute drive to Cape, but when she wanted to, Mom could make it much faster.

Later, Daddy told me that as he sat there on the steps crouched in pain, he was praying. He asked, "God, I just got all these wonderful new toys. Could I have just a little more time to play with them?" The Lord heard and granted his prayer - he passed away about a year later.

Daddy at Cape Rock, Circa 1934.

Daddy recorded the eight-track tapes to cassette tapes for me. You would listen to three minutes of music and then hear the gearing shifting on the eight-track, followed by another three minutes of music. I appreciated all his efforts but our taste in music had diverged.

Somewhere in the box of tapes I saved is a recording of Grandpa Linebarger and Daddy swapping jokes. Another has a conversation between Daddy and my then three-year-old son Jamie deciding whose buddy Jamie was. Jamie vacillated between being Grandpa's

Daddy and Mom. Circa 1970.

buddy or Daddy's buddy, depending on who prompted him last.

When I was in the marching band, Daddy came to all the football games. He didn't sit in the stands, but walked the sideline on the opposite side of the field. Other people's kids got equal treatment. Any young player at the city park who asked Daddy to come watch him play had a new fan to cheer them on at their next game.

At the park, Daddy noticed all the empty soft drink cans being thrown on the ground and began to pick them up in a bag and take them home. He had decided to start selling aluminum cans to local vendors. He drove a big station wagon at the time. When people heard he was cleaning up the park and making a little money, they collected cans for him, too. He'd come back from watching a game to find the station wagon covered with empty cans.

One morning he was sitting outside on the top step at the side door tying his shoes. When he stood up, he lost his balance. As he fell, his elbow broke the glass in the storm door behind him and he was seriously cut. Doctors warned that he might not regain full use of his right arm as a result of the damage to nerves, muscles and tendons.

Aunt Rose, Daddy and Mom at the side yard swing. Jackson. The A-frame for the swing came from a child's play set. Daddy drove an iron pipe through the top piece so it couldn't collapse from the weight of several occupants. The swing itself is one he made. There is also a sheet-metal screen over the top for protection from the birds.

He found a little hand machine, much like an old-fashioned nut cracker. It was fastened to a surface and using its handle much like pumping water, jaws would close on an object and crush it. He began to crush all those soda cans with his injured right arm. It took a long, long time, but he regained all the muscle in his arm, one can at a time.

The city park service was now aware that Daddy was gathering cans and getting therapy by crushing them. The city council awarded him a proclamation for his good deed to the city. They even offered to take his cans to whatever market he wanted to cash them in. Big mistake.

On the appointed day, a large flat-bed truck pulled into the driveway to load the bags of cans. Daddy had phoned all around and the best price being offered was in Sikeston, MO, forty miles away. The crew was astounded; they thought this little errand would be completed by mid-morning. The basement and garage were so full of bags of crushed cans it was necessary to weave one's way to the shower or washing machine. They filled the entire truck bed. It wasn't heavy, but there was lots of it.

My husband and I accompanied the truck to Sikeston and collected over $500 for the cans. Then we had to give the fellows a twenty for gas to get back to Jackson and buy them some lunch. We all went to Lambert's, home of the famous "throwed rolls."

The "throwed rolls" label began when a fellow was having lunch at Lambert's, which was always packed, and wanted a hot yeast roll (they are delicious). The server couldn't get to him through the crowd. The fellow called, "Just throw me one." Someone else hollered, "Me, too." Soon rolls were flying all over the restaurant to hungry diners. It became their signature move and continues today.

Daddy sang and played at Eastern Star and Masonic meetings, picnics, bunking parties, White Shrine, in the kitchen, side steps, front steps – anywhere a crowd wanted to gather. Hubert Bollinger beat on a piano and sometimes Johnny Crites played accordion with him. He said grace at most events that required a blessing. He sang at funerals, weddings, and special occasions. He never refused to oblige and I don't know of a single instance when he accepted any payment other than a heartfelt "thank you for that, Everette."

I often joined him, especially on "This Old House" by Rosemary Clooney. We had a repertoire of songs where I sang the echo, repeating his first phrase several measures later. I really amused my folks one morning when I sang "Sixteen Tons," a new piece by Tennessee Ernie Ford, for them.

Daddy often sat in the side swing with a scrape of wood and his pocket knife whittling. The item he cut the most was the word "keys." Adding few cup screws and staining the wood created a great key holder. He made and gave away hundreds and hundreds of them.

Hymns were favorites of Daddy's, "Old Rugged Cross," "Amazing Grace," "Let Your Lower Lights be Burning," "How Great Thou Art," and "In The Garden."

Mom said the last time Daddy sang it was "How Great Thou

Last photograph ever taken of Daddy at an Eastern Star meeting.
Circa Oct., 1990.

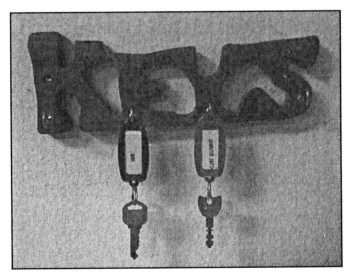

Daddy's whittled key holder.

Art" at an Eastern Star meeting. He told her, "I was running out of breath; I didn't think I was going to make it, Pete." The photo above was taken that night. He passed away less than a week later.

139

DESEGREGATION

I don't recall why Mom and I were on a bus in Cape Girardeau, but that's where I saw my first Negro person. I sat down between Mom and the lady, staring at her in wonderment. I recall reaching over, brushing her hand with mine, and then examining my fingers.

She smiled and said, "It's alright, Sugar, it doesn't rub off."

Mom was appalled! She grabbed my hand and gave it a shake because I had violated another person's space without invitation. The lady just nodded at us, I believe she recognized the innocence of my

Typical visit 1976. Mom and Daddy's nest. Daddy playing fierce with Jeff (5), Kim (15) in foreground, and Mom with Jamie (11), Jackson.

curiosity. But I didn't get another smile from Mom until much later that day.

When my son Jamie was in school, he had a social studies assignment that involved parents. He asked me to recall the most significant event I could from the 1950's. I told him that one morning in 1952 my fourth grade teacher announced that the new President of the United States was Dwight D. Eisenhower. However, that didn't hold a candle to what occurred a couple years later: desegregation of the public schools.

I didn't particularly understand why everyone was talking about desegregation during the summer I was eleven. It seemed to worry people a lot and I was warned by total strangers to be on my guard. It was suggested that I let my fingernails grow so I wouldn't be defenseless, but I didn't know what there was to fear. This was all baffling to a child who hadn't been raised to be biased, prejudiced or ignorant of the world.

Prior to desegregation, the Negro children had a separate school building for all grades. Their students were absorbed into the white school without incident. I have no idea what happened to their teachers, none of them came to the white schools to work.

Our class got Bobby Mitchell. Bobby was older than we were and bigger. I didn't like it when my teacher, Mrs. Mills, asked him to read aloud because he was not good at it. I was embarrassed by his discomfort. I appreciated that she never did that again.

Bobby wasn't in our class the following year. He was double-promoted several times in a row. That was necessary because if he hadn't been, he would've reached age twenty-one before he graduated high school. At that time, no one over twenty-one years of age could attend public school.

Bobby grew to be a very handsome man and an outstanding athlete. Because of his prowess in football, he was revered by his fellow students and despised by opponents. If anyone could get the football in Bobby's hands, we had a touchdown, or rather, another touchdown. There were bounties on him – if an opponent could put him out of the game, it was worth a forty-nine cent milk shake. We really did live in the sticks.

Mom regularly came to the home games to see the marching band perform. She sat in the bleachers where supporters of the opposing team would caution her that people like Bobby would marry her daughters. Mom had a withering look that could silence any antagonist and such remarks were not repeated.

Daddy admired Bobby's abilities as much as anyone else. As the ball advanced or fell back, he re-positioned himself appropriately on the field sideline, smoking Camel cigarettes all the while.

Years later, Daddy ran into Bobby uptown one day. They exchanged news about their families. Bobby told him that he'd always liked me; I'd been nice to him. Bobby said that the only mistake I'd ever made was to marry my first husband.

Judy – first grade.
That's Mom's handwriting.

I am from collie dogs that raced free in the meadows and litters of kittens that magically appeared in the grain shed.

When the city folks tired of a pet, it was taken for a one-way trip to the country. Often, thirsty animals padded their way from the highway to our farmhouse to beg for a drink of water.

Jeannie showed up at the farm just that way. She was a beautiful, shiny black German shepherd with rust and white dressing. Since we didn't know where she came from, she was named Question Jeannie. Her puppies were born on Mother's Day.

What fun to throw a rope in with that furry bunch for a game of tug-of-war. 1949 on the farm.

We had gone to Grandma Linebarger's, dropping Grandma Looney off at Aunt Grace's on the way back. When we returned home, it was nearly dark.

Barking with excitement, Jeannie came running, then spun and dashed toward the barn. When we didn't follow, she repeated the routine. Daddy handed Jo a flashlight and told her and June to go

June, Judy and Jo, plus eight puppies. 1949 on the farm.

see what had Jeannie so worked up. Daddy said if she had birthed the puppies and any were female, he'd have to kill them.

Jo and June followed the dog to the barn and crawled under the large manger. They found a bed Jeannie had made back against the wall with eight puppies in it. They flipped over each puppy and returned to tell Daddy, "Ha, ha, you can't kill them; they all have 'dinks.' They're all boys."

Daddy said, "You didn't look closely enough." He took the flashlight and went to look himself. Sure enough, they were all male, and all collies with no trace of their German Shepherd mother. Looking more like Lassie than Rin-Tin-Tin, each puppy had a tuff of white on the end of its tail.

One afternoon soon after the puppies were born, Jo and June had climbed the cherry tree and were playing on the roof of the brooder house. Suddenly, Jeannie began to tear circles around the building. Mom called to them to stay on the roof; Jeannie had worms and was having a fit. Still crazed, Jeannie raced down the driveway into the road and was promptly hit by a passing car.

The irony of this event was how seldom a car passed on that

*Judy with Cousins Gail and Carol Avery. That's the grain shed
behind us. It was important that I wear a coat outside – it was not
important that the coat fit or be buttoned. . Circa 1950.*

highway during the mid-day. But Jeannie had dashed in front of that
very "seldom" car.

The woman driver came to the house and told Mom she'd hit a
dog that ran out in front of her. Mom asked if the dog was dead. If
so, she'd have to kill the puppies. (Farming is a life of hard decisions.)

The woman said Jeannie was lying in the road but wasn't dead.
Mom got gunnysacks from the grain house and together she and
the driver were able to get Jeannie onto one. They moved her on the
floorboard of the woman's car and drove to the house. Mom had Jo
and June help her carry Jeannie to the puppies for them to nurse.
When the puppies were full, they carried Jeannie back to the house.
Mom put down a pan of bacon grease for Jeannie and she ate it all.
Several hours later she got up, wobbled to the barn and lay down
with her pups. A few days later, she was fine. And, no more worms.
If a dog had a fit of any sort, Mom cured it with a meal of bacon
grease.

Several months later, Aunt Eula and Uncle Hollin visited from
Cape. Daddy made the mistake of mentioning that the puppies were

Jo, June, Cousins Gail and Carol, Prince,
Butchie, and Judy. Circa 1950.

weaned and he would be killing Jeannie. Aunt Eula was horrified and demanded that she take the dog with her. Daddy's reasoning was that we didn't need any more puppies and a female dog was an over-population problem waiting to happen. Aunt Eula eventually found a home for Jeannie on another farm. Repeat, farming is a life of hard decisions.

A lot of leeway was afforded the pets on the farm, but if a dog killed a chicken, it took a one-way walk to the woods with Daddy. Jo had a little dog named Timmy that killed a hen. She spent the morning trying to find him. Finally Daddy had her sit with him on the cistern step and told her that he had to take Tim back to the place we'd gotten him from. No – Daddy had taken that little chicken-killer for a walk.

The puppies were temporarily divided among us. Then neighbors took several pups, and one that Daddy didn't see was killed when he backed over it as he left for work one morning. June was chasing one of hers with the rotary lawn mower when the puppy stopped short. However, June didn't. Thereafter, he was known as Bob-tail. We ended up with two adult dogs: Prince and Butchie.

While we were at school one day, Butchie came to the house agi-

146

Jo, Judy, June with a dog, Cousin Glen Gearing with a dog, Gail and Carol Avery in wagon with Cousin Buck Drum kneeling behind.

tated. He barked, ran away, came back and barked again. Mom filled her apron pockets with scissors, wire cutters, a knife, and tools for every contingency she could predict she's find.

The dogs must've been jumping barbed-wire fences. When Butch led Mom to Prince, he was completely tangled in the barbs. Mom spent hours cutting his long coat to get him free. She got him to the farm and watched as he crawled underneath the house to die.

When we pulled a small toy wagon, the collies would fight to get to ride in it; only one would fit. June could make a yelping sound that would summon the dogs to us, knowing the wagon was in motion. After we got home from school, we tied up Butchie to keep him in place. Then June paced back and forth in front of the opening to the crawl space pulling the empty wagon. It took a long time, but Prince finally struggled back into the yard. Mom caught him, doctored him, and gave him a bowl of bacon grease. In Mom's opinion, bacon grease could heal any animal. At least that was true with Prince. In no time, he was once again racing through the tall grass in the meadows with Butchie.

The grain shed was a free-standing building where kittens would suddenly appear. They were placed in a bushel basket to protect

147

One of the farm cats sat on top of the garden gate post and watched Mom through the kitchen window. When Mom started toward the cistern steps, where scraps were left in bowls, that cat was first in line.

Daddy farmed for many years with a span of mules, but he eventually replaced them with horses, Toots and Johnny. They weren't draft animals but I recall them as being huge. Daddy once found me playing among their powerful legs. I was fine, but Jo and June got a spanking for not watching me. I don't remember that, but I smile as I type it.

Beware of little sisters.

Baby chicks were bought every year and put in another free-standing building, the brooder house. A stove kept them warm until they reached maturity. In the summer, it became a playhouse. Once my folks got a new mattress and we used the empty box to divide the area into rooms. We were living high.

I am from two siblings –
one that taught me to read
and one that taught me to fight.

Jo would hand-copy pages of the *Dick and Jane* readers at school. At night, she'd lay her papers on a kitchen chair seat and we would kneel on the floor. She would laboriously go over and over each word with me, pointing patiently with her forefinger. She did it again and

From the left, Skipper Kelly, June holding Cindy Kelly, Jo holding Ricky Schneier, and Mom. Jackson living room. Circa 1959.

again until something clicked. She had taught me to read.

Reading is still an activity I long for and make time to enjoy. Finding a book so intriguing that I truly don't want to put it down is a rare and satisfying event. And it all started with Jo.   A short walk down the blacktopped surface of Old Cape Road, just past Jenny Ruzzel's store, a steep gravel street descended to a footbridge across Goose Creek. Lush trees lined the creek and provided shade to serious crawdad hunters during summer vacations. Ruth Ann and I enjoyed lifting rocks in the creek and watching the crawdads scurry for safety beneath an adjacent stone.

Often we stopped on the way for a bottle of pop at Jenny's. Hers was a very small grocery room, separated from the rest of her house by a draped curtain across a door. Her store carried milk, bread and other essentials, plus a variety of small items. Especially ice cream. I straightened her miscellaneous merchandise table by the front window while we waited for the school bus in winter. There were Band-Aids, emery boards, aspirin bottles, thimbles, thread, etc.

The wonderful thing about Jenny was that if you were short of cash, she would literally "put you on the wall." It was my first credit account. A small piece of paper that said: "Judy owes $0.05" was pinned to the wall. My dad stopped for several Pepsis every few days, and if I was lucky, he bought me off the wall. (My IOU was taken down.)

Ruth Ann and I spent many blissful hours playing in the cold water, not bothering anyone, not disturbing anyone. However, one eventful day some older boys approached the creek from the opposite side, which was an undeveloped open area with few houses in the distance. They began to throw stones at us. Boys!

We moved out of range and kept our mouths shut, until the largest boy picked up a huge rock and hurled it at me. It hit my ankle and really hurt. I screamed and began to cry. He laughed and shouted, "How's that for a hit?"

Ruth Ann helped me hobble home where I sobbed my mournful tale to Mom as she applied ice packs to my swelling ankle. I couldn't get my shoe on next morning and had to stay home from school. (Smile.)

Jo and June asked who the boy was but I had no idea of his identity. I described him and June nodded like she knew who I meant.

June seemed to feel she had proprietary rights concerning me. She could twist my arm, pull my hair, pinch, scratch and generally boss me around – but no one else could.

Armed with the description of my assailant, she waited until the school bell rang dismissing study hall which was situated in the second floor library. For the girls, study hall was an opportunity to do class assignments or use the reference materials that lined the walls. For the boys, it was an opportunity to look for photographs of bare-breasted native women in *National Geographic* magazines.

Jo and June in front of the grain shed on the farm. That's the farmhouse in the background. Circa 1949.

As the class dismissal bell rang and everyone started getting to their feet, June walked up to the boy I had fingered and slapped him upside the head as hard as she could. As she did this, she asked, "How's that for a hit?"

June reported that the boy's face turned four shades of red, except for the vivid white outline of her hand on his cheek. His friends backed away in mute wonder and the villainous boy spoke not a word, just curled his tail under and slinked off.

It is good to have a sister on your side.

My envy of Jo and June's bicycles had no limit. Jo would sometimes permit me to push her bike around in circles in the yard. When I misjudged its weight and it fell away from me, with me on top, I scurried to get it upright before she discovered I might have harmed it. I washed off lots of grass residue. June, on the other hand, simply forbid me to touch her bike.

When I finally got tall enough to get my leg over the bar, the father of two daughters had bought them boys' bicycles; Jo tried to teach me to ride. She would get me on the street and then run beside me holding onto the back of the seat to steady me while I struggled to reach the pedals. Valiant tries but tiring for Jo.

To my astonishment, one day June led me to the top of the hill that ran down by Jenny's store. I got on the bike and June gave me a shove. It was wonderful! I was flying! Then I was flying faster! John Ritter, the neighborhood paperboy was crossing the street. We panicked when we saw each other.

I screamed, "Run."

John did. In a blur I continued past him off the road, hit a barbed-wire fence that flipped me and the bike into Charlie Tripp's front field.

Struggling with that heavy cumbersome bike, still substantially larger than me, I lugged it back up the hill. June was waiting for me with an I-could-have-told-you-that-was-going-to-happen smirk on her face.

I said, "Let's do it again – but first, show me the brakes."

Ole June couldn't fool me; she loved me.

SMOKEY, THE DOG

Judy and Smokey on the Jackson front porch. Circa 1955.

I was playing around Harry Talley's big cattle truck when it began to storm. The massive tires raised the truck about four feet above the ground and I decided to shelter from the rain beneath it. It was a pleasant surprise when a buff-colored dog had the same notion and
crawled underneath from the opposite side. We spent the time getting acquainted until the rain stopped.

I knocked on Carrie Talley's door; she was accustomed to my visits, and asked her for a rag. It didn't occur to me to go home and get a rag, but she gave me one. I tore it into strips and fashioned a collar and leash out of it. I tied my new dog to the faucets in the basement while I ate supper.

When Daddy came home and saw Smoke, short for Smokey, he untied him and ran him off. Each morning I'd whistle up Smoke and feed him left over biscuits and gravy. I knew how to adopt a dog.

It was extremely important to me that Smoke have a rabies shot. I missed Prince and Butchie, the collies, *huge* as they had remained on the farm in spite of my protests. I felt that a rabies shot would indeed make Smokey mine and I asked Daddy to take us to the vet often.

Smokey at home. Jackson, circa 1955

Daddy would say "I'll give him a shot. I've got a rifle upstairs in the closet." Ah, he was starting to get used to Smokey.

Eventually we made that trip. The vet identified Smoke as a Spitz breed, he carried his tail above his back in a half curve.

From the outside, Smoke could open the hinged door between the garage and the basement by pushing it with his nose. Daddy nailed a large empty sewing thread spool to the inside bottom of the door. When he wanted out, Smoke would slap the spool with his paw and the door would bounce. He'd keep it up until the door bounced open wide enough for him to zip through.

Daddy's friends would often ask to borrow a snake, a tool to open a drain, or an over-sized wrench. Daddy would tell them the garage door was open to just go into the basement and get the tool.

Judy and Smoke. Jackson.

They would later report that the fierce dog guarding the entrance and wouldn't let them in. Smokey had employment.

Mom would tolerate Smokey walking through the kitchen but then he was immediately relegated to the basement. No dogs in the house.

It was not unusual for Smokey to disappear for several days at a time. I suspect he had another family somewhere, like a traveling salesman. One morning I heard him crying and checked the side door. Smokey was standing in the yard with a very large trap on his

155

right front paw. The trap had a chain that ran to a second trap that had been sprung. A metal circle connected the traps, which were toothless. The traps were designed to be secured to the ground. I have no idea how Smokey got the traps loose.

I told Daddy what was happening and he went outside to where Smoke was waiting. He sat on the steps and started talking softly to him. When he picked up the trap on Smokey's foot, Smoke began to

Mom made the clothes I'm wearing in these
pictures. Jackson, Circa 1956.

lick his hand, repeatedly, and hard. Daddy squeezed the trap open and Smokey's foot slipped loose. Smokey continued to lick Daddy's hand while I got him something to eat and water.

Thereafter, Smokey would be running through the yard on all four feet and spot a family member. Up would come the right front paw and he would struggle over for a little pitiful loving because of his poor wounded leg, which had a permanent crease over the top of it from the grip of the trap.

Homer O'Neil, our city policeman, would sometimes have to wave Daddy down and tell him that his dog had been uptown peeing on the courthouse shrubs again. Smokey ran free and lacked discretion.

One day Daddy took Smokey with him in the truck to the junk yard. They got out and Daddy emptied the truck bed. When he was ready to leave, he couldn't find Smokey. He drove the five miles home and as he turned into the driveway, he saw Smokey coming up over the hill to the house from the opposite direction.

When Jo and June were invited to a neighbor girl's party and I was excluded, it was Smokey that comforted me. He was a faithful companion to a lonely and confused little girl.

Smokey was a fine boy; a real gentleman.

Grandpa James Edward Linebarger

I am from a blind street sweeper who was part Cherokee Indian.

The summer I was twelve, Grandpa and Grandma Linebarger's live-in caretaker, Miss Platt, wanted to go on a trip to Europe. She would be away for six weeks. Everyone was concerned regarding who would look after my grandparents. Mom said, "Judy can take care of them." What's that? Huh? Mom was clearly out of her mind.

James – April 4, 1877 – September 21, 1959
Ida Mae – July 25, 1881 – August 8, 1955.
Both at Sedgewickville Cemetery.

I couldn't even make coffee, let alone meals. It was horrible but I took Miss Platt's place. Grandma was mean. She didn't like the way I did anything, and said so repeatedly. Grandpa kept his distance.

Laundering the bedclothes was an all-day affair with metal tubs pulled into the converted bathroom from the back yard. The washing machine was an old wringer style that balked at squeezing water out of anything thicker than a washcloth. Just hanging dripping

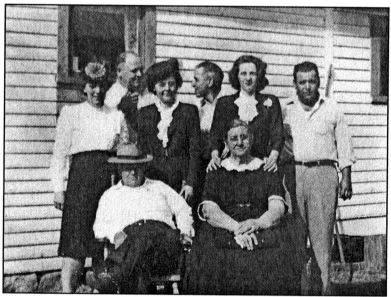

The Linebarger brood – Front row - Grandpa and Grandma, behind them, Eula, Oma, Golda, back row - Limey, Howard and Everette (Daddy).

items on the clothesline to dry was an arduous. My cousin Donnie came and helped me but it was a monster job that neither of us knew how to do.

Grandma weighed over three hundred and fifty pounds and was on crutches. I thought she'd been crippled by illness or accident but later learned that her legs simply couldn't support her weight. the little house out yonder and installed bathroom fixtures in an existing bedroom. There was one-step down into the

When city sewers were installed, the homeowner did away with

The Linebarger children. The girls in the front row: Aunt Oma, Aunt Golda, Aunt Eula, the second row fellows: Uncle Limey, Uncle Howard and Daddy. Grandma's house, Cape Girardeau, circa 1947.

bathroom. When Grandma could no longer negotiate the step, Daddy built her a super strong potty chair. Every morning I had to carry its' slop pot to the toilet and empty it, rinse it with water from the tub faucet, and pour in a little bit of Clorox. Ugh!

A side porch room had been closed off with plastic sheeting. When the wind stirred, the plastic moved so that the room seemed to breathe. There was an ancient wind-up Victrola in there that had one record and one needle. Side A was a laughing record. It started with a tee-hee, then a snicker, a chuckle, an outright guffaw, until it developed into a rolling belly laugh that went on for some time. It was contagious, I couldn't help laughing. Side B of the record was "Carolina Moon." By the time I listened to each side five or six times, I'd hear Grandma yelling, "Judy, stop playing that record!" Grandma was generous with her gloom.

While Grandma napped in the afternoon, Grandpa and I sat in Adirondack-style chairs he'd built on the side yard. We'd play Twenty Questions - Animal, Vegetable or Mineral, or what color will the next car through the intersection be? And if I was really bored, which occurred often, I'd color the half-moons on Grandpa's fingernails with a lead pencil. I looked forward to this time every day. It

Grandpa Linebarger in the Adirondack chair he built. Cape Girardeau.

On their porch, 236 Pearl Street, Cape Girardeau.

was the highlight that balanced the melancholy.

Grandpa had a brother, Harvey Linebarger, the man with the scary milky eye. He would visit the farm and try to be friendly, but all I could see was that sinister eye.

It was summer time, which meant all the windows were opened. I had to dust each morning but by mid-afternoon, soot from the shoe factory smokestacks had once again settled on all surfaces. Mom would walk over from the shoe factory every few days and visit me, but she wouldn't take me back home no matter how hard I begged.

Grandma had cooked lunches for the shoe factory workers for many years until she could no longer manage to do the work.

A bowl of shredded wheat cereal and milk went into the refrigerator each night so it would be soft enough for Grandma to eat for breakfast. Once that summer, Grandma sent me to the grocery to buy a cake mix. It was like she'd finally noticed I was there.

In the evenings, the neighborhood children played in the street beneath the lamps. Grandma didn't believe the world was safe

Grandma Linebarger and Mom on Grandma's porch, Mom hugging her handbag, ready to run for it and leave me there. Pearl Street, Cape Girardeau, 1955.

beyond her front fence so I was forbidden to leave the yard. When they got too loud Grandma would yell at them from the porch. One boy always defied her. She'd yell, "Rocky Beerswald, I'm calling the police on you!" Everyone knew it was a hollow threat and went right on with their business of being kids.

D. B. was an older cousin that Grandma had raised along with her own children. Years before, her brother John came by and dropped D.B. off and never came back for him. As an adult, he would often come to Grandma's to sleep off the alcohol he'd consumed the night before. D.B would go to the kitchen and peel an onion. He'd stand at the sink and eat the onion like an apple. Then he'd go upstairs and go to bed. I kept my distance since he gave off an unpleasant mixture of smells.

I got my first period while I was there. I told Grandma there was something wrong and she immediately understood. She sent me to the chifferobe in her bedroom where I took out a large suitcase. I opened it to find another suitcase inside. There were four more suitcases nested inside each other. The final suitcase held a bottle of Mogan David wine. She filled the bottle cap and had me drink it. I put all the suitcases back together and was sent to bed. Grandma hid the

Four generations. Jo on Great Grandma Frances Hilderbrand Linebarger's lap, wife of William Lafayette Linebarger, Grandpa James Edward Linebarger on the left and Daddy on the right. Circa 1940

Jo on Great Grandma Frances Linebarger's lap with Uncle Howard's children. Cousin Joy Lee on the left and Cousin Delores (Chicken) on the right. Circa 1940

wine because she was afraid D.B. would find her little stash of liquor.

There were some standard rules about a girl's behavior during her monthly period. No jumping off the porch and no shampooing one's hair. The furnace vents in our kitchen were near the ceiling, so if one was in a hurry, it was necessary to stand on a chair in front of the vent. And turning up the furnace to continue the air flow was not an option.

Daddy said he was about nine when the family moved from Sedgesville to Cape. The Sedgesville shack they lived in had cracks between the boards. They stuffed the cracks with old newspapers or mud to keep the cold out. Grandpa got a job hauling debris, trash and tree limbs in Cape, so they moved.

Grandpa Linebarger had the ability to pull up poison ivy without contracting it. He'd pile it up and burn it for neighbors without any ill effects from the smoke. This trait did not pass down to later generations.

The Cherokee Indian bloodline came through Grandpa Linebarger down through the Hildebrand side. We are related to the Cherokee Princess Otahki buried in the Cape Girardeau Trail of Tears Park. She died during the force march that killed so many of her tribe in 1838-1839.

Grandma couldn't breathe well if she laid flat in bed. About two dozen pillows at the head of it propped her so she could sleep sitting up. When she got sick, the family rented a small derrick that was supposed to lift her from the bed and pivot her to the potty chair. She was really more than the derrick could handle and it usually took two people standing on the derrick's feet to keep it from tipping over.

Grandma passed away at the end of that summer of heart failure. Aunt Oma had been at her bedside and said Grandma kept pointing to the chifferobe, but there wasn't anything in there but luggage. I told her what Grandma had wanted was a sip of that concealed Mogan David wine to stimulate her heart.

Frances Linebarger was the daughter of Sam Hildebrand.

Grandma left me a length of lilac patterned fabric that Mom made into a skirt. After Grandma passed away, sometimes on Sunday Daddy drove to Cape to fetch Grandpa to our house. He'd have dinner with us, and then he and Daddy would play checkers. Every once in a while Grandpa would suddenly sweep the checkers onto the floor and scold Daddy, "I'm playing to win! Don't *let* me win!" They'd play the next game as though there had been no interruption. After supper, Daddy would take Grandpa home again.

When Daddy built the Jackson house, he left one nail only partially driven in. He handed a hammer to Grandpa and said, "Finish it up, Pop." Grandpa was very pleased and smiled as he drove home the last nail, satisfied that he'd helped build the house.

By the time I was in fourth grade, I had developed a fascination with pocketknives. I don't recall how it started, but one day during physical education class in the gymnasium, we tumbled on thick blue rubber mats. After doing somersaults, I walked back to the mat and picked up the four knives that had fallen out of my blue jeans, two in each front pocket. I recall buying one at the dime store, but you could buy just about anything there. I once bought a .22-caliber

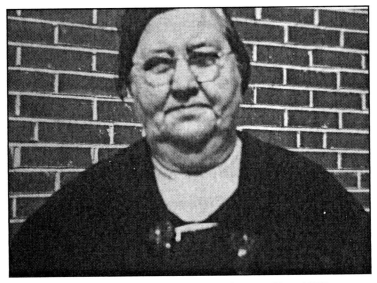

Grandma Ida Mae Cook Linebarger. Circa 1955.

Aunt Eula and Grandma Linebarger, occasion, location and date unknown.

rifle at the drug store, and as an adult, bought tequila at the grocery store. I didn't make the purchase, but a still was available at the hardware store to make personal consumption moonshine.

We had a fugitive relative that would slip into and out of Missouri to visit the family. There was an outstanding warrant for her arrest, the result of a gross miscarriage of justice. Even the sheriff thought so, because he would call Grandpa Linebarger and tell him that my relative had been spotted and she best get across the Mississippi River before he arrived in Cape to serve the papers on her.

On one occasion we visited my family member in Illinois. We stayed in a motel. Incredible – a motel. I can't believe Mom and Daddy paid for accommodations. I'm surprised we didn't strike a tent on the motel lawn.

I was curious when I spotted a corner what-not shelf high up on a wall of the motel room. I climbed up on a chair and examined the carnival-like figurines positioned there, then noticed something small and black propped in a shadow. It was like a tiny book, about one by two inches, with a black leatherette cover. Turning the pages, it was quite ordinary; pictures of a woman. However, if the pages were flipped, the woman undressed. Flipped in the opposite direction, she dressed again. Bonanza!

Months later, I managed to get Grandpa alone and showed him my newly found treasure. He flipped the little book one direction then the other for some time. Finally he asked, "What do you want for it?" Grandpa had a lovely switchblade knife with a pearl-inlaid handle.

I suggested a trade for the coveted knife. Grandpa loved to debate a good swap and we discussed the transaction in detail. At last he went to his bureau and pulled out the knife, depositing the little book in its place. It was a win-win.

I never saw that little book again, I wonder if it still exists.

Grandma and Grandpa's house. That's me running into the photo.

The Bushyhead Memorial,
Cape Girardeau, MO. Photo 2016.

Bushyhead Memorial plaque, Cape Girardeau, MO. Photo 2016.

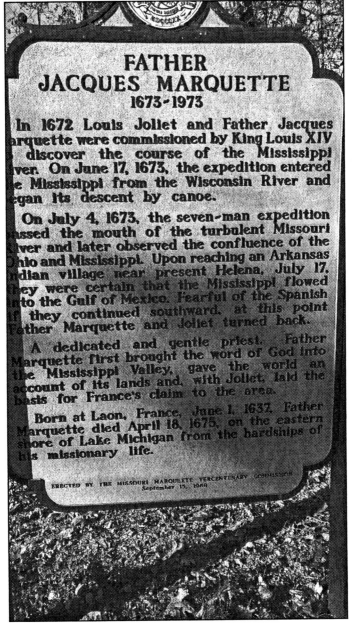

Sign near the Bushyhead Memorial. Photo 2016.

Hannah A. Seabaugh Hartle, mother of Mary Edith Hartle Looney.

I am from a young bride left to raise her six younger brothers when their mother died.

Grandma Looney was the second of ten children and the only girl. Her brothers were Willis, Curby, Robert, Jesse, Jefferson, Lucia, Ode, Edward and Fred. Jesse and Jefferson were twins. Jeff died from spinal meningitis when he was twenty. On the way home from the funeral, Great Grandma Hannah Hartle came down with the same disease. They managed to get her to a neighbor's house where she died.

After her mother passed, Great Grandpa Simon Peter Hartle depended exclusively on Grandma Looney to help raise her six brothers, the youngest Fred, was four. Great Grandpa would bring Grandma a bolt of fabric and tell her how many shirts the boys would need for school and she was expected to sew them. When she talked about her youth, she would bitterly tell about watching her brothers run and play in the fields while she made a meal or sewed clothing.

Grandpa Looney siblings were Benjamin, Cora and Carrie. Cora married Willis Hartle, which gave Mom four double-first cousins.

Alexander Hamilton Looney and Mary Edith Hartle were married January 4, 1897. They rented a farm on Little Muddy Creek in Bollinger County, Missouri for eleven years. Aunt Grace was a baby when they moved there. In 1910, Grandpa had an opportunity to purchase a one hundred forty-four acre farm for $1,600 on Highway 61. Mom was born nine months later in the wheat house. Mom was two or three when construction on the big farmhouse was complete. Grandpa brought Grandma to her new home in a horse-drawn sleigh after a snowstorm.

Mom remembered construction of the house. When the men were digging the cellar, Mom was continually drawn to it. Although she was warned away, she persisted. The workmen would pick her up and swing her over the deep hole that became the cellar. Yeah, that would keep her away.

During the Little Muddy Creek farm years, Grandma suffered with a malaria-type illness and chills. This condition was due to the humid climate near the creek and she regularly took quinine to relieve the symptoms. Upon leaving Muddy Creek, the malaria ceased being a problem and Grandma abandoned taking quinine. At a quilting bee a few months after moving, a friend confided to Grandma that she had heard that quinine was a natural contraceptive. Knowing that she had ingested quinine for her illness for eleven years, an astonished Grandma exclaimed, "It certainly was for me!"

That might explain why there were twelve years between Aunt Grace and Mom. After

Mary Edith Hartle Looney at age 3. Circa 1875.

Grandma Looney sitting on Uncle Ode's car bumper. Circa 1930.

174

Mom was born, Grandpa was called in to see her. He suggested that she be named after her two grandmothers, Catherine and Hannah. In the German influenced community, her name would've been pronounced Han-nar Cat-a-rine, which Aunt Grace didn't like.

Grandpa stomped out of the room and said, "Name her what you want; I'll call her Pete."

Although formally named Rita Marie, throughout her life Mom remained Pete to everyone who knew her. During early school years when a boy dared to call her "Reater," she felt compelled to wrestle him to the ground and explain his mistake because her name was, after all, Pete.

A photo of Hannah Seabaugh Hartle hung in the living room on the farm. It disturbed us as children because her eyes followed us around the room. Christian Seabaugh, Hannah's father, had eight children with his first wife who died. He remarried and had eight additional children. Great Grandmother Hannah Seabaugh was among the first eight children. Although some moved away, most of the Looneys stayed in the Nashville area.

Daily, Grandma Looney walked down the long gravel driveway

Grandpa Looney with his mules, Kate and Old John.

175

Hannah A. Seabaugh Hartle

for the newspaper and the mail. Prince and Butchie, the collies, accompanied her. Butchie liked to carry the newspaper back for her
in his mouth. By the time they reached the back door, the paper was
thoroughly wet. Consequently, Grandma carried the previous day's
newspaper with her to the mailbox to give Butchie so she could pre-
serve the new one.

A friend of Grandma Looney's lived nearby. When she'd an-
nounce to her family that she was going to visit Edith, (Grandma),
they'd say okay, but you have to wear shoes. She'd put on shoes and
as soon as she was out of sight, she'd take them off and carry them

Grandpa Looney with his mules, Kate and Old John.

Grandma is second from the left in front of the farmhouse.

177

Grandma Looney with Jo on the right and June on the left. Circa 1941.

to Grandma's. She loved to regale Grandma with stories liberally sprinkled with cuss words. Jo and June stuck tight when she visited. If they didn't already know the cuss words, they would learn a few new ones while she was there. Later, she would walk back home, stopping near her place to put her shoes back on.

A niece of Grandma Looney's showed up at the farm with her young man. Her folks had thrown her out. She was pregnant and needed a place to stay. She was wearing the only clothes she had. Grandma and Mom got busy cutting out fabric and sewing her dresses. After a few days, Grandma asked her if she and her husband had decided what they were going to do. The niece said, "Oh, we're not married." Within an hour they were both trudging down the driveway.

Grandma was incensed. The new unreliable telephone system only worked sporadically and the niece's folks had tried to call but couldn't get through. They'd been searching everywhere for her.

We moved into the house in Jackson over Thanksgiving of 1950. A few days later, we were eating breakfast at the kitchen table when Grandma threw her sweater onto the back of her chair. She commented that the weather outside must have warmed up significantly. Daddy was amused when he told her that it was furnace heat rather than cook stove heat making the room toasty.

The last years of her life, Grandma Looney lived six months with Mom and six months with Aunt Grace in Cape.

In March, 1951, Grandma died of a heart attack.

Grandpa, Mom and Grandma Looney Alexander
Alex - August 12, 1872 – January 30, 1939
Mary Edith - October 17, 1872 to March 25, 1951
Both at Sedgewickville Cemetery

Grandma Looney holding Jo. Circa 1937. Did I mention Jo was born with a full head of hair?

Jo, circa 1937.

From left, June, Grandma holding me, and Jo. On the farm, circa 1945.

I am from mashed potatoes smothered in gravy and bacon five times a week.

As I grew older, Christmas remained exciting. My stocking (a sock) held the same items each year – oranges, hard ribbon candy and walnuts, secretly filled Christmas Eve by Santa. Mom left the bowl she'd transported these items in on the coffee table so we could put them back as we emptied our loot.

Occasionally, we were permitted to open one gift before the 25th. Serious evaluations were made as to which of the wrapped packages we each would open. I shook and hefted mine trying to decide which held the greatest treasure.

Finally I made by decision and chose a square box. I saw Mom and Daddy exchange a look. Mom was running back and forth to the kitchen cooking supper - stir this and salt that. I wondered if they were going to say wait until after we eat.

Nothing was said, so I opened my gift – a miniature gray plastic water tank about eight inches high with a nozzle on one side for filling a toy steam engine train. I was puzzled and sputtered a thank you. Again, Mom and Daddy exchanged a look and said 'you might as well open this other one.' The other one was an electric train. Hot damn! Daddy split some electric wires and connected the power box to the train and we all started playing.

When we reminisced about that Christmas, it was always: the year Judy got the train and Mom burned the potatoes for supper.

Daddy and Aunt Grace, Christmas, Jackson. Circa 1960.

*Typical Christmas. Alene, Vicki, Mom, Skipper and June.
Ricky on the floor. Circa 1960.*

MOM

As a little girl, Mom went everywhere with her dad, and he never missed anything. The entire trip he'd point things out to her: yonder were a pair of gray rabbits, that's a chicken hawk circling over Wilson's woods, notice the broken corn stalks where something big has crashed through, weather's getting cool, time to trim the saplings. She developed unusual powers of observation that proved a hazard once I started dating.

I sucked my thumb as a child; it was just always in my mouth, where it belonged. I was ambidextrous - it didn't matter whether it was the right or the left one. It was never tolerated and always discouraged.

Mom was constantly putting something that would burn my tongue on my thumbs, but I'd wipe it off with my shirt tail. At some

The Thumb Sucker with June sitting on the cistern steps, circa 1949. To the left is the garden gate. In the far distance to the left, the barn. Behind June, Mom's cauldron for washing clothes is boiling away.

Mom beside the farmhouse. Wonder whose shadow that is? Circa 1922.

point I got both thumbs infected and a doctor had to lance the sores. After so many failed remedies to make me stop, gauze bandages were effective. By the time my thumbs healed, I'd forgotten that I liked sucking them. Then one day Jo and June reminded me. They said, "You used to do this," and showed me how it was done. Talk about an outraged mother! I sat watching her yell at my sisters while serenely sucking my delicious thumb.

As a new incentive, Mom offered to reward me with a quarter for each day I didn't suck my thumb. It was an amazing bargain, twenty-

A Woman-Not –to-be-Messed-With. Mom, Jackson, MO. Circa 1955.

five cents that was all mine. We were still on the farm, so I was very young, but old enough to realize that money could add up. Mom never had to worry when she gave me the quarter each day. She'd wait until I'd been to bed for about fifteen minutes and then walk in and whisper, "Give me your thumb." She'd feel of it, and of course, it was moist! She'd slip her hand beneath my pillow and retrieve the quarter.

Sometime after we moved to Jackson, I added my forefinger to the habit. Suck one thumb, clasp my own wrist with the other hand, and pat the palm of my hand. No idea when I actually stopped - maybe after a boy named Dickie kissed me in the darkness of the Saturday afternoon matinee.

Mom had a wreck with the old '49 Mercury in Millersville. We had been to a dinner of some sort and Mom had a plate she'd made up for Daddy in the back seat. The contents scattered everywhere. I was shocked and alarmed when she turned to me and asked if I was all right – her mouth was bleeding. I'd never seen blood on Mom

Mom is the second woman from the right, standing next to Cousin Buck.

The front end of the car was smashed in, but it still functioned, so it was not repaired. When someone asked, "Pete, what happened to your car?" Mom would answer, "The termites got into it."

We went to visit Irene Bollinger one afternoon. We usually played with Idona and Alta Faye, but now they had Danny, a new baby brother. Jo and June were lugging him around and noticed that his diaper was wet. His mom said, "Go in the house and change him." Jo and June had never seen how a boy was made and by the time they finished, there wasn't an inch of that little guy that hadn't been carefully inspected.

Mom said, "It sure is taking them a long time to change one baby."

Irene responded, "Don't worry; they're probably just checking everything out."

Jo would play with Alta Faye's little dog, Nero, when he visited our farm on his own volition. He'd lie on his back and let her rub his belly, play with his toes and gently tug at his tail. But when she squeezed his testicles, Nero got up and went home.

Mom made all our dresses and underwear. She sewed clothes to

188

fit June, who was slightly bigger than Jo, even though Jo was older. Eventually, June grew out of the clothes and Jo grew into them, or Jo just wrapped them around her body and wore a belt.

When Mom got annoyed, she would disappear. I could ferret her out and usually found her sitting on the side of her bed playing Solitaire. Being a helpful child, I would contribute to her game by pointing out plays she was missing. Somehow my assistance made her snap the cards as she laid them down.

Daddy and Mom at Cape Rock Drive. Cape Girardeau, circa 1934.

Ella Bingheimer and Mom on the posts by the Jackson Cemetery gates.
Jackson, Circa 1924.

After the move to Jackson, the folks bought an electric washing machine. It had a tub with an agitator and a wringer. The wringer had two rollers that compressed a garment and squeezed the water out of it as it fed between the rollers. The wringer had a release bar that Mom would beat when it began to "eat" clothes. She used the stick from the barn that she had used to smack a calf under the chin, reminding it to stay on his side of the cow's udders.

Once a Jackson city work crew was driving by and saw my elderly mother on her hands and knees in the front yard. She later said she was simply working in the grass and couldn't get her feet beneath her - she couldn't get up. So she was crawling to the steps to leverage her way to her feet. The crew jumped out and assisted Mom to the front door, ushered her into the house and closed the front door.

The front door had a half-moon glass at the top. Mom stood on tip-toe looking through it as she watched the men leave. Then she opened the front door and went back to her work in the yard.

As Mom grew older, I telephoned her every day during the drive

Mom is wearing a rose pin on her blouse. I often borrowed it to wear while I was home. Unpacking after one such trip, I found the rose pin on top of the items in my suitcase. Sweet Mom.

Mom on the left, with Uncle Robert Hartle's children, Alfred and Ermel, circa 1913.

home from work. She had a specially issued phone from Missouri Bell that was ear-splitting loud. If she didn't answer right away, I might let it ring fifty to seventy-five times, it took her awhile to get to it.

After one such wait when the phone had been ringing forever, I asked if I had pulled her away from something important. She said no, the yard had just been mowed and the   grass looked so pretty she'd gone outside to walk in it. When she came into the house, she could hear the telephone ringing. She had damp grass clinging to her bare feet, so she'd gone to the bathroom to wash them.

I asked if she stepped into the tub and ran water over her feet? She said no, she stuck her foot in the toilet and flushed it. Then she stood on a towel and put the other foot in the toilet and flushed it again.

I was dumbfounded! Ingenious. That was Mom.

Daddy at Cape Rock.

 DADDY

Daddy was a friend to everyone. He was always helping people that needed his strength, his counsel or his bravado. Sometimes it was working for a relative who promised cash for a laborious job but instead pawned off a piece of junk in payment. Sometimes it was helping a stranger, neither expecting nor receiving anything for a helping hand.

One such instance of his generous nature was the day there was a sound like a sonic boom and a helicopter made an emergency landing in the cornfield across the highway from the farm. The engine suddenly stopped running and the helicopter plummeted toward the ground, landing safely through the pilot's efforts. It was a beautiful bright blue color.

We weren't allowed to cross the road but Daddy went to check on the pilot, who was unharmed. The pilot knew which part he needed

*Mom and Daddy on the right with friends at Cape Rock Drive.
Cape Girardeau.*

to repair the helicopter, so Daddy drove him to town to get the necessary piece at the hardware store. Late that afternoon, the pretty bird lifted off. No rides were offered by the pilot and none would have been permitted by my folks.

The pilot was trying to find Millersville. Mom told him to follow the highway south and he'd see it some five miles down the road.

Daddy worked for fourteen hard years on the farm. Until Grandpa's death, his advice or suggestions were always ignored. Grandpa Looney knew he was sick, dying, and felt he had but a few months to teach Daddy everything he needed to know about farming; they didn't need to try anything new.

When an offer was made to buy the farm, Daddy was more than ready to move to Jackson. He was working for Albert Sanders Hardware store responding to requests for plumbing and heating services. The twice daily fifteen-mile commute wasted a large portion of his day.

Eventually, he bought the truck and equipment from Sanders and established his own business. I don't know the year but the accelerator was shaped like a table spoon.

After I got my driver's license at age sixteen, he would permit me to drive the truck to school. Our driveway was quite steep, so backing up a hill while trying to master a clutch and straight-transmission was tricky. Not really tricky, more like riding a bucking horse. Once at the top of the driveway it was necessary to maintain the gas/clutch action to check for traffic in both directions. Poor Daddy endured those jerking, twitching, convulsing rides for months before my coordination kicked in. I'd see his head bouncing forward and back while I pretended to be getting better at driving. Eventually the old truck went to his oldest grandson, Skipper, who painted it candy-apple red.

Years after my parents built the house on Old Cape Road, my sister Jo and husband Dale bought the old Albert Sanders house, where they were raising five children. At one point, they all were teenagers. (Scream!) Rick turned nineteen around the same time

Leslie turned thirteen. Sis, Boo and Scott were in between.

Only two back yards separated Jo's house from Mom and Daddy's and a path was worn by the children traversing from place to place. In those days, children were tolerated for being children. Mom was still working at the shoe factory in Cape, so the kids spent their time with Daddy, and Daddy spent his time in the garden.

Daddy would clear and plow the Jackson garden in early spring. One had to wait to plant until the earth warmed a little after the winter cold. After planting, he'd tie poles in a tepee shape for the green beans to climb and carry out the tomato stakes to be handy when needed. The children were welcomed in the garden, but could only dig where Daddy indicated. If he caught them digging elsewhere, a chase would ensue. Daddy was a large man, but he could run! He'd grab his big stick and chase the grandkids across the backyards

That's Daddy's truck in the background. Jo on our neighbor Mable Henderson's glider. We didn't go into Mable's yard, but when Jo married Dale Schneier, Mable became her aunt by marriage. Otherwise, Jo would not be lounging there. When Mable defrosted her freezer, she'd invite me over to eat all her melting ice cream. I liked Mable. Jackson.

*Daddy. Those are Mom's forget-me-nots against the house.
Circa 1955, Jackson.*

and up their back steps and into their house. Screaming, they'd hide beneath the kitchen table and beg Jo to save them from Grandpa's wrath. Jo was always successful in protecting her brood from the mock savage waving the stick. Daddy would lean over and ask, "Are my eyes green? When I get angry, my eyes turn green." (Daddy's eyes were green.)

The only other garden rule was to walk in Daddy's tracks. He didn't want them to trample the earth he had already plowed, so they had to step where he stepped. First would be Rick, stepping carefully in the tracks Daddy had made. Then Vicky (Sis), then Boo. It was a little more difficult for Scott and Leslie to match the stride, so they jumped from footprint to footprint. Better to work harder than be expelled from the fun of Grandpa's garden.

The neighbors would sit together in the backyard under a shade tree and watch this procession of Daddy and the kids. They often joked, "Everette's shadow is getting longer every year."

When it was time to harvest, the kids were in the thick of it. As Daddy picked pole beans, a little garter snake would stick his head

Daddy on the left, making music and having fun on Cape Rock Drive.

Daddy's high school graduation photo. Circa 1932.

Mom and Daddy on the rear right side, Cousin Buck standing on the left side. Cape Rock.

out. It bothered Leslie, but Daddy would just push him back into the plants. The snake would accompany Daddy down the rows of beans, popping his head out often. Leslie wanted Dad to get rid of him. Daddy said the snake was his friend, Bruce, and Bruce ate the bugs off the green beans. He was glad to share the garden with him.

Being extremely strong, Daddy's hand had the strength of a vice. He would let Jo, June and me see that he was putting something in his palm. Money. It might be a nickel, a fifty-cent piece, a $5 bill. Then the challenge - we could have it if we could force his hand open. We didn't even have to go one at a time. We all three pounced, raising one finger at a time to get leverage on another. The finger would suddenly curl, perhaps trapping one of our own that had to be wrenched free. We stepped on each other, climbed on Daddy for a better vantage point, tickled him. We were forbidden to bite. Didn't matter; we never opened his fist.

But it was much funnier when he played the same game with the grandchildren.

Daddy was generally a healthy man all his life, but he was claustrophobic. Maybe it was because he was a large man, but put him in a small space and he started sweating bullets. He had to crawl beneath many houses to do plumbing work. He always told his helper, "Never get between me and the daylight." The dirt, cobwebs and dead rodents didn't bother him, but if his helper blocked the light while Daddy was under the house, Daddy would barrel right over him to escape.

Prior to the St. Louis Cardinals moving to Phoenix, AZ in 1987, Daddy and two of his friends, Bill and John, made the rare trip to see them play at Busch Stadium. On the way home, they stopped at a well-known steakhouse for supper. They all gave the waitress their orders. Daddy's was always "knock off the horns and hooves and drive it on in."

John went to freshen up and while he was away, Daddy and Bill conspired against him. They called the waitress over and informed her that they were caretakers from an insane asylum. (There was such a facility in nearby Farmington.) They explained that John

Daddy's "shadow" makers. Children Boo and Sissy Schneier seated on the floor, next row, Chris and Jeff Kelley, then Cindy and Skipper Kelley, Scotty Schneier on Daddy's right knee, Leslie Schneier on his left and Ricky Schneier beside her. Jackson. Circa 1966.

had escaped and they were on their way back to the hospital with him. Although normally John was not dangerous or unruly, he had missed several days of medication. In view of that, in order to avoid an unfortunate incident, under no circumstances should the waitress give John any silverware.

A long afternoon in the sun cheering for your favorite team can produce a mighty appetite. John returned to the table rubbing his hands together in anticipation of enjoying his steak dinner. After serving everyone, the waitress turned to walk away. John called to her that she'd forgotten his silverware. She glanced at Daddy and

203

Bill, who gave her a knowing look, and she told John he couldn't have any silverware. He insisted. He demanded. He pleaded. He begged. He threatened. He sulked. He picked up the steak with his hands and ate it.

There is something about a farm that attracts city folks. During the summers, invited and uninvited company appeared.

The Tinker family of St. Louis, with their six or eight kids, came every year for four days at a time. The boys were put in Jo and June's beds, which they peed, perhaps deliberately. The rest of the kids slept on featherbeds on the floor. The primary rule for the boys was to stay away from the horses. Bright and early the first morning, the boys took some ears of corn for bait and slipped off to find the horses. Soon someone missed them and asked where they were. Daddy knew which field the horses were in and he and Mr. Tinker started out to find the boys. Everybody else trooped along with them.

We passed a stream that ran through the farm where Weeping Willows flourished. Mr. Tinker cut a long branch about half an inch thick. He vowed that if he found his boys with the horses he would whip their hides off. Everyone heard his declaration.

Soon they were approaching the boys who were trying to get on one of the horse's back. Mr. Tinker seemed to regret his impulsive statement, but the boys and all the rest of the children had to be taught a lesson. He really laid into them.

Another year when the Tinker family came, they brought a monkey. It was a nasty hissing thing that managed to escape its lead and climb a tree. Everyone surrounded the tree so the monkey couldn't get down and escape into the woods. Hoping to coax him down, June held her hand out with some shelled corn in it and called, "Would you like some corn, little monkey?" The monkey promptly leapt from the tree at June, landed in her hand and bit her thumb. They left that day and never returned.

Mom always made Jo and June stay with the kids to play, but they were hateful children that wouldn't cooperate. I asked Jo what relation the Tinker family was to us. She had no idea. She added that they were a bunch of smart-ass, whiney, bored, city kids.

In more recent years, Jo stopped in Jackson at Wib's drive-in for a sandwich. She sat at the counter with several other men customers that she soon realized were "regulars." They were joking and laughing to the point she felt comfortable asking, "Did you ever know Everette Linebarger?" Oh, sure, they knew Everette! They proceeded to tell her story after story of how every time they saw Daddy he had another riddle for them. Hard riddles; riddles they could not solve. I don't know where he was getting them, but Daddy did love riddles. The things you learn about a parent by accident are amazing.

One of the most terrifying days I can recall as a child was May 21, 1949, the day the tornado went through. Jo, June and I were sitting with Grandma Looney in the car outside Scharper's IGA. Our folks had picked us up from the movie theater and needed a few grocery items before heading for home.

Uncle Robert, Grandma Looney's brother, and Aunt Nancy Hartle.

Rain was pouring down so the car windows were rolled up. It got very hot inside the car and suddenly Grandma's nose began to bleed. We held her handkerchiefs against the window glass to make them cold so they could serve as a compress against Grandma's sinuses and brow. It didn't help much but did slow the blood flow.

Driving back to the farm, we didn't know there had been a tornado. We came over a rise about a mile from home and saw cars pulled onto the shoulder of the road. Daddy walked down to see what had happened and returned with the news that the top floor of Jesse and Rainey's brick house was gone, taken by a tornado. As we hurried home, Daddy turned on the car radio and heard that a tornado had hit Cape Girardeau, causing extensive damage.

That morning, Grandma Looney had set a bucket of newspapers to be burned by the cistern. When we arrived home, the newspapers were still dry. It hadn't even rained at our place.

Our folks didn't bother to do the milking; they just instructed Jo and June to put the calf into the stall with the cow, let the calf have all the milk, and headed for Cape.

It was two very frightened little girls that stumbled to the barn to tend to the calf. Although we were with Grandma, we didn't know what a tornado was and were scared it might come back and get us.

Grandma and Grandpa Linebarger had huddled together in the middle of their living room while the tornado passed over. When Mom and Daddy walked in, Grandpa said, "We wondered how long it would take you to get here."

Aunt Grace and my cousins were hunkered down together as well; scared that they were going to get hit because the noise was so loud and close. Aunt Oma's house had minor damage but her yard was torn up. Several hundred residents were killed.

Later reports indicated that the tornado was aimed directly for our farm when it suddenly veered and hit Jesse and Rainey. They repaired their house but never replaced the second floor. Rainey wanted Mom to help her put up new wallpaper, something Mom knew nothing about, but they got the job done.

After all those years on the farm watching the sky, Daddy was quite adept at reading it. Farmers always knew if it would storm the next day. Even now, I can smell it on the wind when rain is coming.

When he saw a black cloud approaching in Jackson, he'd instruct us to head to the basement. Inevitably, Mom would go open the front door and look out for herself.

Daddy would say, "Woman, if it was here you would be gone now."

Daddy would stand just outside the open garage door until he gave an "all clear" that it was safe to resume life.

One July Daddy had a rainy day experience almost as interesting as the tornado. It had been raining hard for several days so the fields were too wet to work the ground. Daddy decided to visit Benjamin Franklin Hartle, Grandma Looney's brother. As he approached the house, Daddy noticed smoke coming from the chimney. Uncle Frank and Aunt Jane had a fire going in the living room stove, in July! Daddy knocked at the door and Uncle Frank gruffly called out, "Who is it?" Daddy told him it was Everette, and Uncle Frank opened the door, holding a gun in his hand.

Aunt Jane was ironing money. They had to light the stove in order to heat the irons. Twine was zig-zagged across the rooms and money hung on it to dry. Daddy walked around

Aunt Jane and Great Uncle Frank Hartle, Grandma Looney's brother.

marveling at the sight and couldn't help noticing that the bills were not ones or fives, but of large denomination.

Many country farmers of the era didn't trust banks and kept their money at home. It was usually put in a glass jar or wooden box and buried by a particular fence post or beneath a certain tree.

Uncle Frank kept his money buried in a tin can, which had leaked. Thus, Aunt Jane was ironing the money dry. He often wanted to show Daddy where the money was buried, but Daddy didn't want to know. Perhaps it's still there.

As often happens when distracted by never ending chores, at some point, our farm cats had multiplied until there were twenty to twenty-five of them running around the farmyard. Tossing table scraps into the yard after meals caused an immediate eruption of squabbles as each cat vied for a share of the bounty. The only other food they received was in the barn when a bowl was squirted full from a well-aimed udder as the cows were milked. The cats earned their keep by thwarting the mouse and rat population from doing their best to invade the grain bins.

One morning Daddy carried his shotgun to a harvested field and threw handfuls of corn on the ground. Soon a flock of blackbirds fatally pecked at random goodies. One discharge of the shotgun killed twenty-four of them. He carried them home and put them on a table inside the screened porch. As he passed Mom, he told her to have Jo and June feed the birds to the cats, he thought they might have fun with that. Mom was busy and soon forgot what he said.

Grandma Looney walked through the screened porch and saw the pile of birds lying there. She cleaned them and made a blackbird pie for lunch. As we ate, Daddy commented to Grandma that the pie was good and asked what kind of meat it was. She said it was the blackbirds he'd left on the table. Daddy nodded and kept right on eating. Waste not – want not.

At the end of a meal when Daddy got down to a bit of left over biscuit, he'd mix together a little syrup and butter to dab it in. Sometimes he'd complain that he didn't come out even, (a little inventive eating accomplished that), and he'd need to add just a wee bit more syrup to the butter. However, the last thing he had before he left the table was a fork full of peanut butter.

When I would open the peanut jar to make a sandwich, I'd see the tine tracks of all his forkfuls crisscrossing like a railroad yard on the top of the peanut butter. He ate so much, that Mom canned tomatoes in all the accumulated empty jars.

All his life Daddy was prone to drop pearls of wisdom. Daddy's advice to newly married young men: If your wife asks you to dry the dishes, do it, but be sure to drop a cup or plate so it breaks and you'll never be asked again. If your wife cooks a fine meal and asks you how you liked it, don't say it was good – say "it'll do," otherwise you'll have it so often you won't enjoy it. That's when my mother would give me that "he-thinks-he-knows-something" look.

One day while shopping together, Mom and Aunt Grace impulsively decided to have my photo made. That it was not planned is evidenced by my unpolished shoes. This picture was always known as "Judy with the dirty shoes."

I am from steadfast people, loyal, brave and preserving.

On July 4, 1912, Grandpa, Grandma, Aunt Grace and Mom took the horse and buggy to a community holiday celebration at the Methodist Church at Sedgesville. When it was time to go home, my aunt couldn't be found. My grandparents discretely searched for her in vain, and eventually asked everyone to join in the quest. That's when someone noticed that a man named Rosewell Drum was also missing. Fifteen-year-old Grace had eloped. Grandpa Looney was livid. He must have been steaming because my mother, only two

Aunt Hedi Grace Looney Drum
February 8, 1898 – March 3, 1978
Sedgewickville Cemetery
Aunt Grace, for whom I was named.

Aunt Grace and a friend.

years old at the time, remembered his rage.

In a brief time, Aunt Grace had three girls: Lela, Edie and Glendell. Mom was so close in age to her nieces that they were raised like sisters to her. Aunt Grace's husband deserted her and she barely eked out an existence by working at the Brown Shoe Company, which made Forsheim shoes, the finest footwear available at the time. Each shoe came in a pull-string gold velvet bag with a leather emblem embossed with the name "Forsheim."

When Mom was ready to graduate high school, Rosewell liked to taunt Grandpa Looney with remarks like, "Pete can come live with us and go to business school."

Grandpa would fume and reply, "You got one of my daughters but you'll never get the other one!"

Aunt Grace seldom received any financial help from her husband and when she did, he would come by the house and demand to see the receipt for what she had bought.

Rosewell committed suicide in 1932 by drinking carbolic acid. Aunt Grace never re-married; she said she didn't trust bringing a man into the house with all her girls. Mom always called Aunt Grace "my Sis."

Aunt Grace and Mom were doing dishes in the farm kitchen one day while Mom was pregnant with me.

Aunt Grace asked, "What'll you name this baby if it's a boy?"

"James Alexander," Mom answered, "after both grandfathers."

Aunt Grace continued, "You already have a Jo and a June, what will you name the baby if it's a girl? Will it have a J name, too?"

Mom said, "Judith."

Aunt Grace laughed, "You and your J's. What will be her middle name?"

Mom answered, "Grace."

Aunt Grace just smiled and said, "Oh."

I loved to visit Aunt Grace. She had a small house on Bloomfield Road in Cape Girardeau. She lived there with her daughter Buck until Buck passed away. After that, her companion was Bootsie, a small loving dog.

Lelia Oma Drum, "Buck"
June 16, 1914 – June 16, 1955
Died in the hospital on her birthday.
Sedgewickville Cemetery.

Edie Drum Avery, daughter of Aunt Grace, Mom's sister.

I don't know how I got there, but I spent many weekends, arriving on Friday night. Cousin Buck would make a percolator of coffee in their old metal pot on the gas stove. As soon as she turned off the flame beneath it, she poured a cup and immediately drank it. I don't know how she tolerated it so hot. That was her prelude to watching the Friday night fights on television. Boxing matches sponsored by the Gillette Razor Blade Company.

Aunt Grace did not own or know how to drive a car. We would walk to a small local grocery store and she would buy me a bottle of Coca Cola, all for myself. Hog heaven. My own bottle of soda pop, no having to share with Jo and June.

Cousin Edie Avery would bring over her children, Carol Jean and Janice Gail. Carol, Gail and I loved to play together and they would spend the weekend as well. Sometimes Cousin Glendell would also come and bring her son, Rex.

We played a game of clues. An item was hidden, then clues led the one who was "it" to locate the item. Notes like, "look under the red vase." A note beneath the red vase might say, "open the pink candy dish." And so on until the item was found.

Aunt Grace had a little something wrong with the shin area of her leg. She was running through the farmyard and stepped on a rake someone had neglected to put away. The rake tines penetrated her leg and left her a lifetime wound.

Mom said she and Aunt Grace were walking through a field with Buck running around them pretending she was a horse. She kept saying, "Bucky, Bucky."

Ultimately, she became Buck that day.

Cousins Janice Gail
and Carol Jean Avery.

In back, Second Cousin Edie
Avery, next row, Grandma Looney
and Edie's mother, Aunt Grace
Drum. In front, Third Cousins
Carol Jean and Janice Gail Avery.
Circa 1952.

Aunt Grace, around the age she eloped, and years later. In both photos, she is pictured with Uncle Fred Hartle, Grandma Looney's brother.

Cousins Edie and Glen Drum, circa 1924.

Glen and Edie. Circa 1924.

BELOW: Front row: Jo and June. Back row: Edie Avery, Glen Gearing, Aunt Grace and Buck Drum.

Mom and Daddy are in the center of the front row.

I am from Eastern Star meetings and Masonic Lodge halls

Mom was Worthy Matron of the Eastern Star three times and Daddy was Worthy Patron at least once. She and Daddy helped start a local chapter in 1949 in Oak Ridge, Missouri.

When Daddy went to work for T. J. Seabaugh he was put in charge of the deli/meat counter. T. J. asked him to develop a recipe for sausage. Daddy worked at it for a very long time before he perfected a recipe that was satisfying, economical, and delicious. He never divulged the recipe, but volunteered to mix the seasoning in increments – one bag for every fifty pounds of pork.

The Eastern Star at Millersville was renowned for its all-you-can-eat pancakes with whole-hog sausage suppers. Whole-hog sausage used the entire pig, not just certain segments. Daddy's recipe was used to season the sausage. Busloads came the one hundred and twenty-five miles from St. Louis to eat a meal and buy jars of sausage to take home

Mom's Installation as Worthy Matron at Millersville. Ruby Bollinger is to her left.

with them.

The sausage was rolled into balls and baked on huge trays. Leftovers were canned, grease and all.

I carried many, many quarts to Ohio and eked out the supply as long as possible. When Daddy passed away, many well-meaning, (ha – in a pig's eye, I made a pun) - many devious persons tried to persuade Mom to give them the recipe.

Many years prior, there was a family in the Eastern Star that lost their grandfather. The oldest boy came to Daddy and asked if he would be his grandpa; Daddy was honored and agreed. Soon the other kids in the family had adopted Daddy as well. No grandparent was ever loved harder than those children loved Daddy.

When my folks visited me in Ohio, we went to Lake Erie so Daddy could look at a body of water so big he could not see all the way to the other side. Daddy had never seen the ocean either, so when that adopted grandson went to the Atlantic, he set up a video camera to

Jo is at the right end of the first row; Mom is at the left end of the second row. Slightly behind Mom is Johnny Crites, the accordion player, with his wife Velma in front of him. Two people to Velma's left are Ruby Bollinger and her husband Hubert Bollinger, the piano player. The woman third from the left on the front row is Nadia Peak. These people were especially dear friends of Mom and Daddy's.

Mom is in a jacket on the front row receiving her Eastern Star fifty-year pin. 2000.

film the waves so Daddy could see and hear the ocean.

Daddy carried packs of chewing gum, usually Wrigley's Big Red, that he distributed to every child he encountered. His price for the treat was a hug around the neck. Many times he got the hug without the treat, from children and adults.

As Mom aged, she grew concerned about the fate of the sausage recipe. She ultimately elected to give it to one of the girls in the family that had adopted Daddy. Her only proviso was that the recipe was not to be shared and would continue to be used for Eastern Star fund raising events. Her wish continues today.

Eastern Star meetings were as much a part of my young life as Sunday school. I enjoyed watching the activities and being part of the goings on, but was never interested in joining the organization. I'm sure that disappointed both my folks, but I moved away from Missouri by the time I was twenty. They never pressured me for membership.

My parents' Eastern Star Lodge started out in Oak Ridge, Missouri. The meetings were upstairs and the kids were relegated to the downstairs. We listened with interest to the steps overhead as the members marched around in their rituals. Years later, they bought land and built a new Lodge at Millersville. A new member, Rush Limbaugh, Sr., loaned them the money for the project. Mr. Limbaugh enjoyed the fellowship very much, and upon his death, left the deed to the land and building to the Eastern Star.

The new Lodge was a single story building, as Mom, in her nineties, explained, "Those old people can't climb the stairs."

Daddy while Masonic Grand Master.

Daddy bows to me during an installation ceremony in Millersville, MO. I walked from the rear of the gymnasium to the front reading the twenty-third psalm. Circa 1958.

Mom and Daddy – Eastern Star

June, Mom and Jo at the 50-year ceremony.

Daddy, Mom, Ruby Bollinger and two others.

Daddy and a friend at a meeting.

LEFT: Jo and Mom in the living room in Jackson. Jo had also been an Eastern Star Worthy Matron. RIGHT: Mom wearing her fifty-year pin at home. Jackson, 2000.

Walter Howard Linebarger in 1972
Jan 19, 1910 to Mar. 2, 1974
Cape County Memorial Park Cemetery
Daddy's brother.

I am from generations of English, German and Dutch ancestors.

When the Cape Girardeau relatives decided to visit the farm, everyone in the family came along. Uncle Howard's oldest daughter, Joy Lee, would sit in the kitchen and cry.

She was bored and wanted to go home. (Uncle Howard gave her the middle name, Lee, to honor Daddy). His second daughter, De-lores, called Chicken, was right in the thick of things. Nancy Jo, the youngest, played with me.

The fellows would gather in the living room while all the kids played on a wagon outside. Chick asked, "Do you know what the men are doing in the living room? Telling each other dirty jokes, that's what." She then proceeded to tell the kids every dirty joke she knew. She was a prodigy.

As a youngster, Uncle Howard and Aunt Rose's oldest son, How-ard Gene, came to the farm every summer and spent weeks. How-ard Gene was not one to volunteer to work and had not been as-signed chores, so he and Daddy would sit at the kitchen table and play cards.

Observing that Howard Gene did little, Jo and June stopped do-ing their chores, which irritated Mom.

One morning Mom told Daddy and Howard Gene to clear the table, breakfast was nearly cooked. Then she told them again, and once more. Mom removed the burner that allowed fuel to be added to the stove from the top. She walked to the table, gathered most of the playing cards in her hands, walked back to the stove and dropped them into the blazing fire within. Daddy protested, "Why did you do that?" A glance from Mom explained all.

Mom said, "When you go to the fields, take him along and put him to work."

It was the last summer Howard Gene visited.

* * * *

Aunt Eula and Uncle Hollin Pender never had children, and consequently had a gorgeous home and fine furniture. Uncle Hollin worked at the shoe factory and Aunt Eula worked in the alterations department at J. C. Penney's. Aunt Eula sewed beautifully and her workshop at Penney's was a magical place to explore. Since she was a self-avowed expert on all things clothing, she instructed me on how to button my coat, which I thought I'd mastered. She insisted that if the buttonhole was horizontal, then the button should be put through in the same direction. Otherwise, the buttonhole would soon stretch out of shape and be unattractive. It's true.

At home, Aunt Eula had a very modern sewing machine. She would program it to sew, put a brick on the power pedal and head off to do another chore while the machine stitched without her.

Aunt Eula and her sister Aunt Oma sewed peignoir ensembles. They were elaborate with exquisite embroidery and adorned with satin ribbons. They were for, and were used as, their burial clothing. That was back in the days that I had thoughts about things such as that going on around me, but kept those thoughts to myself. By the time I was a teenager, I had outgrown discretion entirely.

Beautiful dolls resided in a basket inside a dining room with elegant glass French doors. She sewed extensive wardrobes for them out of luxury scraps from her Penney's workshop. When I stayed overnight, the first thing I had to do was change the clothes on the dolls. When my younger cousin Nancy Jo visited, she would take off the lovely outfits I had put on them and re-dress them in something hideous. It was an on-going struggle of style and taste.

As a book-of-the-month club member, I thought they were rich. In my young mind, owning books was a wealth indicator, it still is. I usually cleaned for Aunt Eula while I was there. My favorite part was handling said books-of-the-month, which were always dusty. It didn't register at the time that if they were being read, they wouldn't be dusty.

Jo and June often stayed at Aunt Eula's, too. During one winter visit, Aunt Eula insisted they play outside while she cleaned even though it was cold and they didn't have coats with them. After much begging, shivering and trembling, they were finally allowed back inside. While a teenager, Jo was given so many chores to do, for a meager salary of twenty-five cents, that she refused to return.

Mom and Daddy had bought our living room furniture from Aunt Eula and Uncle Hollin. I heard a story that early in their marriage a tearful Aunt Eula came to Daddy and told him that Uncle Hollin

Aunt Eula holding Jo. Circa 1938.

had mistreated her. Daddy had a talk with Uncle Hollin. Only one conversation was necessary.

Uncle Hollin was not very tall and reminded me of a gnome. He liked to smoke cigars, which Aunt Eula demanded he enjoy outside. He admired Daddy and always wanted to help him. Unfortunately, every time Daddy went to step somewhere Uncle Hollin was in the way. When they were building the steps to the second floor in our Jackson house, Uncle Hollin left the hammer on the upper hallway floor. Daddy set me on his shoulders so I could reach the hammer and pass it down to him.

One year Aunt Eula and Daddy decided to raise a garden together. My folks helped plow a large area of land behind Aunt Eula and Uncle Hollin's house and planted it with tomatoes, green beans, cucumbers and such. Mom and Daddy went early in the morning to harvest a mess of tomatoes and were constantly disappointed in the quality of those on the vine. A nosy neighbor informed them that

Eula May Linebarger Pender
Aug. 26, 1903 to Oct. 19, 1991
Hollin N. Pender
Dec. 22, 1898 to Jan. 2, 1998
Cape County Memorial Park Cemetery
Daddy's sister

Uncle Hollin and Aunt Eula were going out even earlier and picking the "cream" of the crop. Daddy built a fence around a section and declared it his. The same neighbor told Daddy that Uncle Hollin was taking a hoe, sticking it through the fence, and knocking off prime tomatoes and rolling them to his side where he could grasp them.

If Mom put her hand on the door to the basement, Aunt Eula stopped her. But Mom was wily and finally slipped down there. Aunt Eula was right behind her hustling Mom back upstairs, but not before Mom sighted her supply of canned tomatoes on the shelves and calculated the number of quarts stored there. Mom was incensed;

she was being robbed.

That's when Daddy plowed a section of our back yard and started planting his own garden again.

Daddy's Big Boy tomatoes were so appetizing and lush that the Holiday Inn in Cape bought them from him when they were preparing for a ladies' luncheon. On those occasions, they were usually stuffed with tuna or chicken salad for the entree.

* * * *

I really loved my Aunt Oma, Cousin Donnie's mother. Her husband, Uncle Lloyd, passed away from a heart attack when Donnie was fourteen. Oma Marada, Daddy's sister, (Jan. 17, 1908 to Apr. 20, 2005) never remarried; I don't think she even dated; she remained Mrs. Lloyd Brooks for the rest of her life. She turned her energies to the church and discovered bridge, which she played with gusto.

I was ten at the time Uncle Lloyd passed, and for some reason it was decided that it would be good for Donnie if I stayed with them for a while. I don't know if I helped to distract Donnie in his grief but I was there. I went with him to the church where he played the organ all afternoon while Uncle Lloyd laid in state. He played all the songs and hymns that Uncle Lloyd particularly loved.

Aunt Oma had decided that Donnie should marry a local girl that she really liked. Then Donnie brought home Uta, a girl he met while living in New Mexico. Uta's folks were German. Our family has a German line in it; however, Aunt Oma didn't like it.

One day while I was visiting, as an adult, Donnie and Uta went somewhere. Aunt Oma grabbed my hand and said, "Come on, we're going to find out about this girl."

I was horrified when Aunt Oma placed Uta's suitcase on the bed and began to search through it. I kept saying things like, "Stop that. This is wrong. Donnie would be very disappointed and angry with you." Man, that woman was thorough. And found nothing.

Donnie happily married Uta.

OMA BROOKS OBITUARY
TUESDAY, APRIL 19, 2005

Oma Linebarger Brooks, 97, of Cape Girardeau died Monday, April 18, 2005, at Southeast Missouri Hospital. She was born Jan. 17, 1908, at Sedgewickville, Mo., daughter of James Edward and Ida May Cook Linebarger. She married Lloyd Given Brooks, who passed away in 1956.

Mrs. Brooks was a shoe dresser at Forsheim Shoe Co. from 1934 to 1975. She was a member of Third Street United Methodist Church, United Methodist Women 74 years, now known as Oma Brooks Society; taught Sunday school more than 60 years, former treasurer of UMW, and was named United Methodist Woman of the Year at the denominational general conference in 2000. She was a member of Eastern Star and a former worthy high priestess.

She is survived by a son, Donald Wayne Brooks and wife Uta of Idaho Falls, Idaho; two grandchildren, Robert Lloyd Brooks and wife Robin of Lewiston, Idaho, Tanya Ann-Marie Brooks Culbreath and husband Bradley of Missoula, Mont.; two great-grandsons, Zackary William and Tyler Wayne Culbreath of Missoula; two nephews, James Edward Green and Howard Gene Linebarger of Cape Girardeau; six nieces, Delores Mary Gerhardt, Joyce Leigh Nussbaum, Carolyn June Kelly and Jo Ellen Schneier, all of Cape Girardeau, Judith Grace Fawley of state of Florida, and Nancy Stone of St. Louis.

Friends may call at Ford and Sons Sprigg Street Funeral Home from 4 to 8 p.m. today. The funeral will be at 10 a.m. Wednesday at the funeral home, with the Rev. Janet Hopkins officiating. Burial will be in Cape County Memorial Park. Memorials may be made to Hobbs Chapel United Methodist Church Elevator Fund.

* * * *

Aunt Golda was Daddy's youngest sister. She was very beautiful and I considered her glamorous. I haven't the faintest idea why she was nicknamed Tillie. As you may have noticed, my family has many nicknames that make no sense.

When she was fifty, Aunt Tillie married a man named Harry Rapp. He adored Aunt Tillie and was one of the sweetest people I ever met. He would answer my knock at their door with delighted smile. He praised how I looked, expressed gratitude for the visit and made me welcome. On a visit with Mom, he immediately went to the kitchen and returned with freshly rinsed nectarines, sharp knifes to cut wedges out of them, and paper towels to catch the drippings.

Aunt Tillie, Golda Marie Linebarger,
Parr, Green, Rapp
July 17, 1915 to Feb. 25, 1998
Perhaps high school graduation.
Daddy's younger sister.

One didn't leave Aunt Tillie's house without a token gift - she insisted. A jewelry babble or an unusual dish, it was always something. Aunt Tillie collected everything. The second floor of her house was loaded with items she loved.

Aunt Eula lived on Independence Street in Cape Girardeau and Aunt Tillie lived next door. When I visited, one would telephone the other and ask, "Guess who I've got?" It was their own style of one-ups-man-ship.

LINEBARGER, RITA M. "PETE" (NEE LOONEY)

Rita M. "Pete" Linebarger
**Visitation: Tuesday, September 21st, between 4-8 PM,
at the McCombs Funeral Home in Jackson**

Service: Wednesday, September 22nd, at 10 AM, at the funeral home

Rita M. "Pete" Linebarger, 93, of Jackson, passed away Sunday, September 19, 2004, at the Lutheran Home where she has resided the past 10 days.

She was born November 15, 1910, in Millersville, Mo., daughter of Alexander H. and Mary Edith Hartle Looney. She and Everette Lee Linebarger were married June 14, 1936, in Cape Girardeau. He passed away October 4, 1990.

Pete and her husband moved to Jackson in 1950 from their farm at Millersville. Pete was a graduate from Cape Business College, and later worked for the former T. J. Seabaugh Grocery Store. She and her husband started The Linebarger Plumbing and Heating Company in Jackson in 1952. At the same time she also worked at the former International Shoe Company in Cape Girardeau for 32 years retiring in 1972. She was a member of New McKendree United Methodist Church in Jackson for many years. She was also a member of the Order of Eastern Star Chapter 310 in Oak Ridge, where she was a past worthy matron and received her 50 year pin in 2000. She was also a member of the Calvary White Shrine #8 of Cape Girardeau, and a charter member of Amarath Court #14 in Cape Girardeau.

Loving survivors include three daughters and sons-in-law, Jo Ellen and J.D. Schneier, June and Dwight Kelley, all of Cape Girardeau, and Judith and Gene Fawley of Pensacola, Florida; 13 grandchildren; three step-grandchildren; 21 great-grandchildren; seven great-step-grandchildren; and one great-great-granddaughter. In addition to her husband, she was preceded in death by her sister, Grace Drum.

Friends may call Tuesday, September 21st, between 4-8 PM, at the McCombs Funeral Home in Jackson. There will be an Eastern Star Service at 7:00 PM. Funeral Service will be Wednesday, September 22nd, at 10 AM, at the funeral home, with Rev. John Rice officiating. Interment will follow in Sedgewickville Cemetery.

Expressions of sympathy may take the form of contributions to the Oak Ridge Eastern Star, Chapter 310.

Uncle Limey (June 25, 1905 to Dec. 9, 1970) and Aunt May. California.

Uncle Limey joined the Navy and was a career sailor. He would rarely visit from his home in California. I only met Uncle Limey once when I was a young woman. He thought I was funny. (As in amusing).

235

Grandpa James and Grandma Ida Linebarger's stone.

Everette and Rita "Pete" Linebarger' stone.

236

Grandma and Grandpa Looney's grave stone. In the distance, the white Methodist church and auxiliary building.

The Everette Linebarger Family: Back row, June, Judy and Jo. Front row, Daddy and Mom. Jackson, 1977.

237

JUDITH FAWLEY

.

GENEALOGY

FROM SEEBACK TO SEABAUGH

1123 – 1988

No records were found in Germany or Switzerland.

1750 is the first year that any records were found in the US. They came from the Historical Society in Lancaster, Pennsylvania.

CHRISTOPHER (SEEBACK) SEABAUGH

Christopher arrived in America around 1745 as an "indentured servant." He served three to five years to "pay his indebtedness" for his ship passage to America.

No records were located regarding where he came from, who might have made the journey with him, how old he was, his marital status, children, or when he passed away.

The approximate date when "One" Son was born, the "Key Ancestor:" Christian Seabaugh born 1749, son of Christopher.

CHRISTIAN SEABAUGH
Son of Christopher Seabaugh

Born 1749 – Died 1835. A will was signed May 1, 1834 and was filed with the Cape Girardeau County Clerk December 3, 1835. Christian married Christina Stotlar in 1771 or 1772. Christian lived in Pennsylvania, then moved to North Carolina sometime between 1783 – 1787. He bought a slave boy named Mike in September, 1808. Christian and Christina with fourteen children and one slave, left North Carolina and arrived at today's Cape Girardeau, Missouri in 1809. Jessie Joseph was the only child born in Missouri. There was a total of fifteen children.

Joseph	Elizabeth	Catherine
Jacob, born 1786	Christian	Peter
Adam	Christina	**Christopher** *
Emanuel	Barbary	Daniel
David	Sally	Jessie Joseph **

* Born 1792
**Born 1809

CHRISTOPHER SEABAUGH
Son of Christian and Christina (Stotlar) Seabaugh

Christopher was born April 1792 in North Carolina – died July 18, 1886. He is buried near Sedgewick, Missouri. Christopher married Mary Elizabeth Hartle, born October 15, 1791 in North Carolina – died December 12, 1891 – buried in Hartle Cemetery, west of Millersville, Missouri. Mary Elizabeth was the daughter of Peter and Elizabeth (Reiter) Hartle. Christopher and Mary had six children:

| Elizabeth | Jesse | Permelia |
| **Sindaline, born 1828** | George | Melvina |

SINDALINE SEABAUGH
Daughter of Christopher and Mary Elizabeth (Hartle) Seabaugh

Sindaline was born in 1828 – died December 21, 1887 at age sixty-two. She is buried near Sedgewickville, Missouri. Sindaline married December 20, 1850 to John Cook, born 1825. John and Sindaline (Seabaugh) Cook had four children:

| Daniel | David |
| Francis M. | **George Washington**, born 1857 |

GEORGE WASHINGTON COOK
Son of John and Sindaline (Seabaugh) Cook

George was born June 23, 1857 – died December 2, 1921. George married August 26, 1880 to Hannah Elizabeth Harmon, born June 21, 1859 – died June 9, 1927. Both buried in Memorial Park, Cape Girardeau, Missouri. George and Hannah (Harmon) Cook had eleven children:

Ida Mae, born 1881	Maude B.	Manerva A.
Mary Jane	Eula Myrtle	Robert L.
Dentis	Andrew Oda	John
Tivis W.	Willie J.	

IDA MAE COOK
Daughter of George and Hannah (Harmon) Cook

Ida Mae was born July 25, 1881 – died August 8, 1955. Ida Mae was married on October 31, 1901 to James Edward Linebarger, born April 4, 1877 – died September 21, 1959.
Both buried at Sedgewickville, Missouri. James and Ida (Cook) Linebarger had seven children:

The oldest boy, Loy, died at age two and was buried at Sedgewickville, Missouri. The grave had no head stone; a gate behind the church was always used as a marker.

Eula Mae, born August 26, 1903 – died October 19, 1991
Erman Edward, born June 25, 1905 – died December 9, 1970
Oma Marada, born January 17, 1908 – died April 20, 2005
Walter Howard, born January 19, 1910 – died March 2, 1974
Everette Lee, born January 9, 1914 – died October 4, 1990
Golda Marie, born July 17, 1915 – died February 25, 1998

EVERETTE LEE LINEBARGER
Son of James and Ida (Cook) Linebarger

Everette Lee was born January 9, 1914 – died October 4, 1990 – buried Sedgewickville, Missouri. He was married June 14, 1936 to Rita Marie Looney, born November 15, 1910. Everette and Rita (Looney) Linebarger had three children:

Jo Ellen, born June 12, 1937 – died
Carolyn June, born June 30, 1938 – died
Judith Grace, born October 19, 1943 – died

*See: **RITA MARIE LOONEY**

JAMES EDWARD LINEBARGER
Son of William Lee Linebarger

James Edward Linebarger – born April 4, 1877 – died September 21, 1959. Son of William Lee and Frances (Hilderbrand) Linebarger.
Brother: Harvey A.   Sister: Alice Linebarger

Medical Histories:

James Edward Linebarger – heart – 220 pounds – cataracts
Ida Mae (Cook) Linebarger – heart – 425 pounds
Everette Lee Linebarger – Diabetic (Insulin) – heart (Large pump ddestroyed by heart attack) – blood clot in leg – 250 pounds.
Rita Marie (Looney) Linebarger – Diabetic (controlled by diet) – thyroid – hearing aids. At age ninety broken leg. Signs of osteoporosis, dizzy. 170 pounds.
Mary Edith (Hartle) Looney – heart – nose bleeds – hearing aids – 160 pounds
Alexander Hamilton Looney – Cancer – stomach or liver. 200 pounds.

JACOB SEABAUGH
Son of Christian and Christina (Stotlar) Seabaugh

Jacob was born in 1786 in Lincoln County, North Carolina. Died July 1, 1833 in Cape Girardeau County, Missouri..Jacob married Sarah Statler, born January 7, 1798 – died November 12, 1878. Both buried at Sargents Chapel Lutheran Church Cemetery, Bollinger County, Missouri. Jacob's tombstone shows he died in 1834; however, he died in 1833. Jacob and Sarah (Statler) Seabaugh had six children:

Henry	Barbary	**Christina**, born 1821
Jacob	Betsy	Catherine

CHRISTINA SEABAUGH
Daughter of Jacob and Sarah (Statler) Seabaugh

Christina Seabaugh was born on September, 13, 1821 in Cape Girardeau County, Missouri. She died September 3, 1891. Christina married on July 23, 1839 to Jefferson Hartle, born May 6, 1818 in North Carolina – died July 21, 1890. Both buried at Sedgewickville, Missouri. Jefferson and Christina (Seabaugh) Hartle had seven children:

Melvinal	Mary	**Simon Peter**, born 1846
Jacob	Jefferson J.	Logan
Nancy		

SIMON PETER HARTLE
Son of Jefferson and Christina (Seabaugh) Hartle

Simon Peter Hartle was born October 9, 1846 – died November 7, 1922. Simon married on April 20 1869 to Hannah A. Seabaugh, born May 20, 1849 – died March 6, 1899, daughter of Jesse and Susanah (Yount) Seabaugh.

See: HANNAH A. SEABAUGH

JESSIE JOSEPH SEABAUGH
Son of Christian and Christina (Stotlar) Seabaugh

Jessie Joseph was born on September 18, 1809, the only child born in Missouri – died May 16, 1895. Buried at Sedgewickville Missouri. Jessie married (1) on July 3, 1831 to Susanah Yount, born 1815 – died between 1853 and 1858. Buried James Cemetery, Bollinger County, Missouri. Jessie and Susanah (Yount) Seabaugh had eight children:

Allen	Mary	John
Christian	Christina	Jacob
Hannah A., born 1849		Eli

Jessie Joseph married (2) in 1858 to Nancy Jo Harmon, born in 1840, Johnson County, Illinois – died in 1871 of smallpox. Buried on the bank of the Little Whitewater Creek in Bollinger County, Missouri. Daughter of Daniel and Martha (Eubanks) Harmon. Jessie Joseph and Nancy Jo had eight children:

Daniel	William	Johnson
Robert E.	Mattie L.	Sarah J.
Albert W.	Minerva	

HANNAH A. SEABAUGH
Daughter of Jessie Joseph and Susanah (Yount) Seabaugh

Hannah A. was born May 20, 1849 and died March 9, 1899 of spinal meningitis. Hannah A. married on April 20 1869 to Simon Peter Hartle, born October 91846 and died November 7, 1922. Both are buried at Sedgewickville, Missouri.

SIMON PETER HARTLE
Son of Jefferson and Christina (Seabaugh) Hartle.
Simon Peter and Hannah A. (Seabaugh) Hartle had ten children:

Willie E.	**Mary Edith**, born 1872	Curby
Robert M.	Jefferson W. and twin Jessie W.	
Lucia J.	Daniel Otis	Edward G.
Fredrick S.		

Hannah was riding home in a wagon from the funeral of her son, Jefferson, when she became ill. She died at a neighbor's farm, never returning home. Jefferson was around eighteen years of age when he died of spinal meningitis. His twin, Jessie, died as a baby. Mary Edith, the only girl, never got to run and play as her brothers did while their mother prepared meals; she always had a baby to tend.

Simon Peter had four sons left to raise when Hannah died. Much of that burden fell on Mary Edith. Simon would take her a bolt of fabric in the fall and she would make the boys' shirts for school for the year. She also sewed the four boys quilts made from their mother's dresses. Frank (Fredrick) never married, so eventually Mary Edith's daughter, Rita, nicknamed "Pete," got that quilt.

MARY EDITH HARTLE
Daughter of Simon Peter and Hannah A. (Seabaugh) Hartle

Mary Edith was born October 17, 1872 and died March 24, 1951. Mary Edith was married January 5, 1897 to Alexander Hamilton Looney, born August 12, 1872 and died January 28, 1939. Both baried at Sedgewickville, Missouri.

Alexander Hamilton and Mary Edith (Hartle) Looney had two children:

Heti Grace, born February 8, 1898 and died March 3, 1978

246

Rita Marie, born November 15, 1910 and died September 19, 2004.

RITA MARIE "PETE" LOONEY
Daughter of Alexander and Mary Edith (Hartle) Looney

Rita was born November 15, 1910. Rita married on June 14, 1936 to Everette Lee Linebarger, born January 9, 1914 and died October 4, 1990. Rita was known as "Pete" her entire life, so named by her father, Alexander H. Looney. Everette Lee and Rita Marie (Looney) Linebarger had three children:

Jo Ellen, born June 12, 1937
Carolyn June, born June 30, 1938
Judith Grace, born October 19, 1943.

Rita Marie Looney, daughter of Alexander Hamilton Looney. Alexander Hamelton Looney, born August 12, 1872 and died January 28, 1939.
Alexander – son of Benjamin and Catherine (Clingingsmith) Looney.

JUDITH FAWLEY

HISTORY OF PETER HARTLE

Peter Hartle migrated from the Palatinate area of Germany, arriving in the port of Philadelphia, Pennsylvania on September 17, 1771, aboard the English ship *Minerva*. According to the ship's passenger list, Peter was the only Hartle transported to the new country in the *Minerva*.

Since the Hartle surname had been present in PA since the beginning of the 18th century, it is most likely that Peter joined relatives who were already in America.

Records indicate that Peter moved on into Lancaster County and then on to Cumberland County, PA, almost immediately, where he acquired a farm just outside the town of Carlyle. He resided in the Carlyle area for the next ten years, excepting a few years spent in Washington County, Maryland, immediately following his first marriage.

On a visit to Washington County, (Hagerstown), Maryland, in 1777, Peter met his future wife, Elizabeth Rieter. They were married there on Feb. 25, 1778, in the German Reform Church, the Reverend Jacob Weimar officiating. The couple remained in the Washington County area until 1780, and then moved back to Cumberland County, PA.

On June 27, 1781, Peter was inducted into the Continental Army via the Cumberland County militia. He was discharged in December 1781, following the battle of Yorktown, in which he participated.

In 1782, Peter and Elizabeth moved on to North Carolina with a number of other German speaking migrants. This movement included five other families with the surname of Hartle. The other Hartle families included the households of Leonard, Joseph, Ludwig, Christopher, and Henry. There are no available records to indicate the kinship of these six Hartle households, however, given the times and circumstances, it is most likely that they were either directly or collaterally connected.

Peter was able to acquire farmland in Lincoln County (Lincolnton) as did the other Hartle families.

Peter's wife, Elizabeth Reiter Hartle, died in North Carolina (no date of death) leaving him with a small son, Simon. Peter next married his second wife, Elizabeth Masters (Meister) in 1795, while still in North Carolina. They had nine children together, three of whom were born in North Carolina, six were born in Missouri.

Circa 1800, Peter Hartle, along with some fifty other German-speaking families, moved on from North Carolina to the Missouri Territory, putting down roots at Cape Girardeau in the deep southeastern part of the territory. The Peter Hartle family was the only Hartle household listed in the migration. It is not clear whether any of the other Hartle families joined the Peter Hartle family in Missouri at a later date. In all likelihood some did. We do know, however, that some remained in North Carolina as evidenced by the spread of the Hartle surname in North Carolina and the adjacent states. It was reported that some went back north and joined other German migrants into the hinterlands of the upper Midwest.

Peter obtained a land grant of some 600 acres located in German township, Cape County, Missouri, where he lived until his death in 1819.

The German families who migrated from North Carolina to Missouri truly found the Promised Land. Land grants of the most fertile soil in America were made to all applicants. The settlers prospered and their descendents proliferated.. Being farmers, families were generally large as a matter of economics. The migrants married off their children to the children of contemporary migrants. This practice continued over approximately 100 years, for at least five generations, to the point where everyone in the community was related to everyone else to some degree.

The descendants of the original families who peopled Southeast Missouri began to move on to other parts of the country around 1900. The Hartle families were no exception and records show that they migrated in small groups, mostly to the West. Most went to the far western states of Washington, Oregon and California. But the telephone book listings throughout the United States attest to the presence of the Hartle surname in all fifty states.

It should be pointed out that the southern branch of the Hartles is not singularly responsible for the dissemination of the Hartle surname. There is a much larger group of Hartles, also emanating from Pennsylvania, who spread the name throughout the north, midwest and far west in the same time frame as that recorded for the southern branch. The tantalizing and ever present question is: are these two groups related? Some say yes; some say no. And there does not seem to be any evidence to settle the matter one way or another. Surely, somewhere, in some long forgotten and obscure writing, there is documentary proof. The writer's intuition, coupled with no small degree of wishful thinking, leans toward accepting kinship as a priority, for lack of evidence to the contrary.

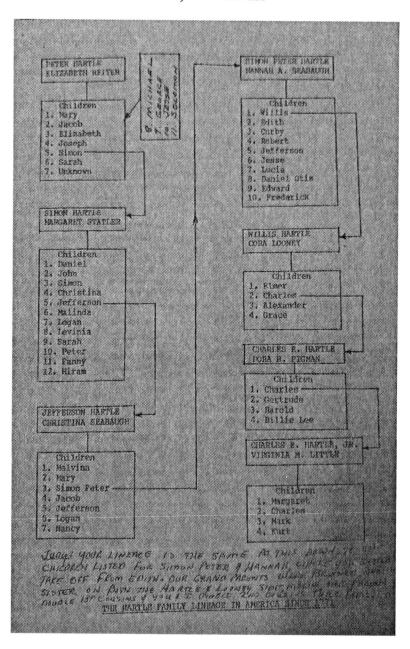

THE HARTLE FAMILY LINEAGE IN AMERICA SINCE 1771

PASSENGER LIST OF SHIP MINERVA
ARRIVING IN PHILADELPHIA SEPT 17, 1971.
PETERS NAME WAS MISSPELLED—OR WAS IT ?

[List 287 C] Before the Honourable Thomas Willing,
Esquire, Philadelphia 17th Day of September 1771.
The Foreigners whose Names are hereunto subscribed, im-
ported in the Minerva, Thomas Arnot, Master, from Rotter-
dam, but last from Cowes, did this day subscribe the usual
Qualification. Consigned to Willing & Morris. 204 Freights.
99 in the List.

Jacob (X) Wentz	Johann Henrich Schmaltz
Henrich Spiess	Geo. Jacob (+) Stultzel
George (X) Miller	Johan Georg Jordy
Joh. Barth. Roehm	Johannes Peter Lütsch
Johann Daniel Schrödter	Philip Müller
Wilh. Fried. Seeger	Christian Knobel
Carl Philipp Ebert	Johann Peter Knatz
Gabriel (X) Gasha	Johann Peter Grissler
Jacob Beier	Johan Friederich Dörsch
Peter (+) Hertel	Johann Conrad Roth
Henrich Schäffer	Andres Gratziger
Henrich Matterkuns	Friederich Dewaldt
Johann Georg Christman	Johannes Best
Henry (X) Dieterich	Jacob (+) Reiff
Jacob (N) Weiss	Christian Gaul
Casper Oker [?]	Nickel Schmidt
Johan Henrich Sche	Johann Conrad Schneider
Conrath Oster	Hans Baltzer (+) Peterman
Johannes Güntlert	Jno. Henry (+) Peterman
Jacob ( ) Young	Johann Philipp Schenckel
Johannes Leynoldt	Jacob Harzer [?]
Michael Pilrege	Anton (X) Glantz
John (—) Werger	Valentin Sash Pfostadecker [?]

JUDITH FAWLEY

List of "Soldiers of the Revolution who received pay for their services," Taken from Manuscript Record, having neither date nor title, but under "Rangers on the Frontiers, 1778-1783" was published in Vol. XXIII, Penna. Archives, Third Series, by the former Editor. (c)

CONTINENTAL LINE.

Hartle, Peter, private.
Harvey, William, private.
Haskey, Robert, private.
Hays, Henry, ensign.
Henderson, John, private.
Hennisey, John, private.
Henry, John, private.
Henry, Robert, private.
Henry, Saml., private.
Henry, William, private.
Heron, David, private.
Heron, James, private.
Hesler, John, private.
Hewston, William, private.
Hill, Asa, captain.
Hodge, Jno., captain.
Hugg, John, private.
Holeman, Henry, private.
Holliday, Samuel, private.
Holliday, Saml., captain.
Holt, Thomas, private.
Hood, John, private.
Horne, Edward, private.
Horrell, James, captain.
Horrell, John, private.
Householder, Fredk., private.
Howard, Samuel, private.
Howard, Thomas, private.
Huy, Samuel, private.
Hufner, Polly, private.
Hufner, George, private.
Hughes, John, private.
Hughes, Patrick, private.
Humphrys, David, private.
Hunter, John, private.
Hunter, Joseph, private.
Hunter, William, private.
Huston, James, private.
Huston, John, private.
Hutchison, James, private.
Hydson, Thomas, private.
Innis, Francis, private.
Innis, James, private.
Irwin, David, private.

THIS IS PROOF THAT OUR COMMON PROGENITOR (PETER HARTLE) SAW SERVICE DURING THE AMERICAN REVOLUTION

254

German Speaking People West of the Catawba River in North Carolina 1750 - 1800

and

Some Émigrés' Participation in the Early Settlement of Southeast Missouri

Compiler and Editor

LORENA SHELL EAKER (Mrs. Odis C.)

Who
Acknowledges with deep appreciation all of those
who have contributed to this effort.

THIS SHOWS THE EXISTENCE OF THE PANTER MINTER FAMILY IN N.C. AS IT IS RECORDED CIRCA 1750 - 1800 & OTHERS WERE BORN LATER IN MISSOURI

JUDITH FAWLEY

LEONARD HART/HARTLE. *Note:* There is some speculation that he was the progenitor of the Hart and Hartle families west of the Catawba, but I found no proof.

On Census and most land records in NC the surname appears under Hart. In estate sales of neighbors, guardians bonds, other miscellaneous records, and some land records, it appears as Hartle, Hartwell, and Hartley, or they signed "Hartle."

In CGC, MO official records show the spelling sometimes as Hart, others as Hartle in the early years. By 1850 everything seems to be "Hartle." Please be aware when researching the name.

What I am including here is a collection of notes that may or may not be one family.

BC, NC Land Entry - 15 Oct. 1778 - Leonard Hart entered 100 A on N. side of Catawba River adj. Joseph Hart/Hartle.

CTC, HB:44, #42 - Martin Keller b. ca 1750 m. Elizabeth Hart/Hartle, dau of Leonard Hartel, and lived Wilkes Co., NC.

LC, NC 1800 Census: Margaret Hartle 1 f. -10, 1 f. 26-45, living next door to Michael Hart.

LC, NC DB 20:104 - 30 Aug. 1800 Jacob Hartle is son-in-law of Conrad Wagner, dec'd. Which Jacob is he?

PETER HARTLE, b. before 1755 MD or PA, d. before Sep. 1819 CGC, MO; m. (1) 25 Feb. 1778 Washington Co., MD Elizabeth Rieter, b. ca 1760 MD or PA, d. ca 1795 or before LC, NC; m. (2) ca 1795 LC, NC Elizabeth Masters, b. ca 1780 or before LC, NC d. 1840-50 CGC, MO., dau of Jacob and Elizabeth Clubb Masters. They moved to MO 1802.

Note: Traditionally Peter had married Elizabeth Rieter but there was no proof. I was browsing through the indefinite loan films at our local Family History Center and located some Maryland records. Their marriage is registered in the Washington Co., MD records of marriages by Rev. Jacob Wiemar 13 Sep. 1777 - 6 Oct. 1786.

BC, NC Land Entries - 27 Jan. 1780 - 100 A entered on Snow Creek.

LC, NC DB 21:86 - 18 Mar. 1802 - Peter Hartle sells 61 A on waters of Howards Creek, part of grant to him 16 Apr. 1785.

1790 Census, LC, NC: 2 m. -16, 1 m. 16+, 2 f. (Only one son, Simon can be accounted for of the children born before 1790.)

1800 LC, NC Census: 1 m. -10, 1 m. 45+, 2 f. -10, 1 f. 16-26.

1 Nov. 1803 CGC, MO. Territorial Record: Peter Hardell 3 m. -14, 1 m. 14+; 2 f. -14, 1 f.

256

Note: Family proved by CGC, MO Probate Records and Court Minutes. One son b. before Nov. 1803 is unaccounted for.

Sources: Records of Thomas E. Kasinger of Alameda, CA, and research of this author.

1A. SIMON HARTLE, b. ca 1779 possibly Washington Co., MD or BC, NC, d. before 29 Sep. 1825 CGC, MO m. before 1800 LC, NC Margaret _____ b. ca 1783 NC d. after 1850 CGC, MO.

2A. MARY HARTLE, b. 1797 LC, NC d. 1891 Bollinger Co., MO, m. 11 Aug. 1818 CGC, MO Christopher Seabaugh, b. 1794 LC, NC d. 18 Jul. 1886 age 92 yr 4 mo 15 da, Bollinger Co., MO.

3A. JACOB HARTLE, b. ca 1799 LC, NC, d. before 19 Jun. 1826 CGC, MO Sarah Ann Smith, b. ca 1799 LC, NC, d. after 1850 CGC, MO, dau of Daniel and Elizabeth Hahn Smith. Sarah Ann m. (2) 24 Aug. 1829 Joseph Miller, son of John and Catherine Miller.

4A. SARAH HARTLE, b. ca 1800 LC, NC d. after 1850 CGC, MO; m. ca 1818 CGC, MO Philip Smith, b. before 1800 LC, NC, son of Daniel and Elizabeth Hahn Smith.

5A. JOSEPH HARTLE, b. ca 1803 NC or MO d. before 19 Jun. 1826 CGC, MO m. 1823-4 CGC, MO Sarah Masters, dau of Jacob Masters. Sarah m. (2) to Philip Wise as his 2nd wife.

6A. ELIZABETH HARTLE, b. ca 1805 CGC, MO, d. before Jun. 1826 CGC, MO, single.

7A. MICHAEL HARTLE, b. ca 1808 CGC, MO d. before Jun. 1826 CGC, MO, single.

8A. GEORGE HARTLE, b. 1813 CGC, MO d. 13 Dec. 1869 CGC, MO; m. 30 Dec. 1830 Mary Niswonger, dau of Joseph and Catherine Limbaugh Niswonger.

9A. JESSE HARTLE, b. 1814 CGC, MO, d. 27 Feb. 1877 m. 5 Mar. 1835 CGC, MO Sarah Seabaugh.

10A. SOLOMON HARTLE, b. 1816 d. 1863 in CW; m. 1 Dec. 1836 CGC, MO Jane Davis.

JOHANN DIETRICH HEFNER/HEAVNER, b. 1723 Germany d. 1787 - or by Jan. 1788 LC, NC m. Elizabeth _____. Was written in records as Tetter or Peter Hefner/Heavner.